Praise for *The Money Habit*

"Mike Michalowicz has a rare gift: he makes complex money decisions feel simple, achievable, and even fun. If you've ever struggled to build better financial habits, *The Money Habit* is for you."
CHRIS GUILLEBEAU, *New York Times*–bestselling author of *Time Anxiety* and *The $100 Startup*

"They want you to believe that security comes from a portfolio you can't understand. The truth is, it comes from within you. This book is the anti-financial advice you should have received, a guide to breaking free from the fear and myths that keep you trapped. You'll learn how to stop trading your freedom for a promise and start building a life of significance and prosperity on your own terms."
GARRETT GUNDERSON, *New York Times*–bestselling author of *Money Unmasked* and *Killing Sacred Cows*

"We used *The Money Habit* to transform the finances of our business and our lives. We can assure you—it works!"
JESSE & EMILY COLE, founders and owners of the Savannah Bananas

"*The Money Habit* gives you the practical, shame-free plan you need to transform your financial life and build a foundation for true wealth."
TIFFANY ALICHE, *New York Times*–bestselling author of *Get Good with Money*

"Your bank account is a reflection of your daily habits, and with this book, you'll learn to transform your financial reality one day at a time. If you are ready to cultivate the discipline, clarity, and control needed to achieve financial peace and success, this is your guide."

HAL ELROD, *USA Today*–bestselling author of *The Miracle Morning*

"I've seen too many people hustle hard only to let their money get away from them. *The Money Habit* gives you the no-nonsense system you need to finally take control and build your riches. Every young and profiting person needs this book!"

HALA TAHA, CEO and founder of YAP Media;
host of the *Young and Profiting* podcast

"If you have wanted to 'Profit First' your personal finances, *The Money Habit* is the book that will show you how."

JUSTIN BENNETT, author of *Level Up Your Finances*

THE
MONEY
HABIT

ALSO BY MIKE MICHALOWICZ

All In

Clockwork

Fix This Next

Get Different

Profit First

Surge

The Pumpkin Plan

The Recession Response (audio only)

The Toilet Paper Entrepreneur

FOR CHILDREN

My Money Bunnies

MIKE MICHALOWICZ

THE MONEY HABIT

The Worry-Free Way to Financial Independence

PAGE TWO
SIMPLIFIED

Copyright © 2026 by Mike Michalowicz

All rights reserved. No part of this book may be reproduced, stored in a retrieval system or transmitted, in any form or by any means, without the prior written consent of the publisher or a license from The Canadian Copyright Licensing Agency (Access Copyright). For a copyright license, visit accesscopyright.ca or call toll free to 1-800-893-5777.

Some names and identifying details have been changed to protect the privacy of individuals.

The information presented in this book is intended for educational and informational purposes only. It does not constitute financial, investment, legal, or other professional advice. The strategies and suggestions outlined herein may not be suitable for every individual, and the reader should consult with a certified financial planner, accountant, or other qualified financial professional to determine the appropriateness of any information to their personal situation. Neither the author nor the publisher assumes any responsibility or liability for any financial decisions or actions taken by the reader based on the information provided in this book.

Cataloguing in publication information is available from Library and Archives Canada.
ISBN 978-1-77458-643-3 (hardcover)
ISBN 978-1-77458-695-2 (ebook)

Page Two
pagetwo.com

Page Two™ is a trademark owned by Page Two Strategies Inc., and is used under license by authorized licensees

Simplified is an imprint of Page Two
pagetwosimplified.com

Jacket and interior design by Peter Cocking
Printed and bound in Canada by Friesens
Distributed in Canada by Raincoast Books
Distributed in the US and internationally by Macmillan

26 27 28 29 30   6 5 4 3 2

mymoneyhabit.com

I dedicate this book to your wallet.

Contents

A Note from the Author About the
Founding Family of Money Habit Mentors *ix*

**Introduction: A Money System That Helped Millions—
Now It's Your Turn** *1*

1. You Have (Already) Won the Lottery *7*
2. The Money Habit System *27*
3. Align Your Money Target With Your Financial Season *43*
4. Plot Your Course on Your Money Map *69*
5. Gain Control with Clarity Accounts *93*
6. Crush Your Debt *119*
7. Build a Better Financial Future Now *141*
8. Embrace Your New Identity *161*

Conclusion: Go Get Your Moments *173*

Acknowledgments *181*

Appendix: Tips and Hacks to Save More Money *185*

Notes *199*

Index *203*

A Note from the Author About the Founding Family of Money Habit Mentors

THE MONEY HABIT is your road map to financial independence. And sometimes, the fastest way to succeed is with a guide. That's where the **Money Habit Mentors** come in.

This trailblazing group of advisors are the first to get certified in my new methodology. They're ready to help you pursue lasting financial stability and build better financial habits. They're not just skilled professionals; I consider them family.

Whether you need clarity, accountability, or a customized plan, this special group of mentors are ready to guide you every step of the way. Your financial independence isn't just a dream, it's a habit. And now, you've got family to help you achieve it.

Moshe Amsel, DreamBuilder Financial, LLC (New York, USA), dreambuilderfinancial.com

Cailyn Meyer, Cashflow Powerhouse (Missouri, USA), cashflowpowerhouse.com

Diane Gardner, Adept Business Solutions (Idaho, USA), profitcoach4you.com

Melissa Garza, By the Book Profits & Financial Management (Texas, USA), bythebookprofits.com

Tatiana Tsoir, Linza Advisors (New York, USA), linzaadvisors.com

NOTE: Money Habit Mentors are part of the Profit First Professionals network, a global community of accountants and bookkeepers on a shared mission to help businesses and individuals achieve financial independence. With their support, your path to financial freedom will be clearer, and far less lonely.

Introduction
A Money System That Helped Millions—Now It's Your Turn

"**OUR PEOPLE** are still living the American Dream, even though they are told they can't have it."

Sometimes, I get feedback from people that floods me with gratitude. Gratitude for the honor of teaching *and* learning. This was one of those times.

Our people are still living the American Dream. In my biggest and wildest fantasies, and I can go big and wild, I assure you, I never imagined I would hear those words. And to receive them, unsolicited, from Travis Snyder, someone who had the data to back it up, well it just doesn't get any better than that.

Travis Snyder is the Dream Manager for A1 Garage Door Service, a company with locations across the United States. For the employees who opt in to the program, Travis's job is to clarify their big life dreams, for themselves and their families. As you can imagine, a lot of those dreams revolve around finances. Paying off debt and buying a forever home are the big ones. A1 Garage Door Service was the first company to introduce the Money Habit system to its employees, because money, effectively managed, is the pathway to those dreams.

It all started with a call I received from Travis's boss, Tommy Mello.

Tommy, the founder and CEO of A1, had read my book *Profit First* and used the system to transform his business into a financial juggernaut. In other words, healthy and huge. Yet, Tommy was worried about the most important part of his company: his employees, all nine hundred of them. While his team of installers and service techs earn higher-than-average incomes for their industry, they still struggled. "Too many of my employees are living paycheck to paycheck and struggling with debt," Tommy said. "Could you come teach them how to use a personal version of the Profit First system?"

Over the years, I'd heard from countless readers who had fixed their business finances with the help of my book *Profit First* but still struggled with personal cash management. I also heard from non-business owners (you know, as in, most people) who had stumbled across the book and were trying to adapt it for their personal lives. Whatever their reason, readers tested the cash management system I shared in that book and found it fixed money problems they hadn't been able to tackle before. It turns out, the principles I describe in *Profit First* work for anyone, whether you are paid hourly or salaried, work part time or full time, are on contract or a permanent employee, are deep in debt or just want to level up your financial game.

I never officially tracked how many inquiries I received, but I suspect it was well into the thousands. I repeatedly told myself, "I'll write that book for personal finance someday." Tommy's call turned "someday" into "today." Plus, there was one person I knew who had already been living both the Profit First system and its corresponding personal finance system for nearly two decades with great effect: me.

Seconds after Tommy's call, I started to assemble all the information, research, and experience I had accumulated while deploying my own simple approach to personal finance. It became the Money Habit system, and it's for people on fixed or flexible incomes, for people who have jobs, or gigs, or side hustles, or passive income, or earn-as-you-churn work, or even own their own businesses. It works with who you are, as you are, wherever you are. But before I share more about it, let me tell you how it started.

I created the original method, the Profit First system, in the early 2000s in a moment of desperation and used it to save my own business, my sanity, and what was left of my bank account. I consider myself ground zero for Profit First, the first person to go all in on the system. And while my business showed the symptoms of my financial ineptitude, the disease was my personal finance. Profit First fixed both.

The system I created is not rocket science and it's not a new idea. To solve my financial chaos, I drew on a method rooted in simplicity, one that had worked for generations: the envelope system.

It works like this:

1 Label a stack of envelopes, one for each type of expense: rent/mortgage, groceries, fun, et cetera.

2 Periodically, allocate a portion of your income to each envelope so you know what is available, for what purpose, before you use it.

3 When it's time to pay a bill or purchase something, use the money in the envelope earmarked for that purpose.

See? Not complicated. You may have already tried this method. Maybe you used jars instead of envelopes. Maybe you stashed money under your mattress or hid one of those jars so well that you @#$%! forgot where you put it.

As with any budget, all these methods work, until they don't. Eventually, you find yourself moving money around between envelopes or jars or dipping into that box under the mattress so you can pay for something you want.

Most budgeting systems fail because they demand new habits that we struggle to sustain. They set us up for short-term success but ultimately leave us where we started, or worse.

Think dieting. We try the new weight loss fad, and it works for a little while, but a few weeks or months later, we're right back where we started, often with even more pounds to lose. The system fails us.

So that's what I set out to fix. I was determined to make a system that was unbreakable, or at least as close to it as possible, for my own undisciplined, marginal-at-math self. I figured out that any transformation requiring you to become someone you're not just wasn't going to work long term, or at all. If I could create something that worked *with* our habits, then we'd be golden. I began my seventeen-year study of human behavior and money.

The Profit First system is the good ol' envelope system, plus the pay-yourself-first principle, married with a remove-the-temptation tenet. And best of all, it works. As in, it *really freaking works*.

I wrote about the Profit First system for the first time in 2008 in a little paragraph in my first book, and then later in an article for *The Wall Street Journal* that went viral. (Not like Taylor Swift–level viral. You know, geeky small business–level viral.)

The first edition of *Profit First* came out in 2014, and we've tracked more than one million implementations worldwide so far. I'm proud to say the system has helped readers break free from financial chaos, set aside money for the little things and the big things, the essentials and the extras, and fund their dreams. I love hearing from business owners who have transformed their finances and are now living their best lives. They send me pictures. Pictures of their family on trips. Pictures of new homes. Pictures of the last debt collection notice in the garbage (or fireplace). And they tell me the good news about how their lives are different, how they can sleep at night, how their mental health has improved, how life just seems easier to handle.

What I love most is that a million-plus people have financial confidence as a result. They are no longer scratching by. They are in control of their cash. They aren't desperate for a lottery win or a get rich scheme. Their cash accumulates while they live life as they want. People who had constant money worries now tell me, "I never have to worry about money again."

I never have to worry about money again. That may seem like a bold claim, but it's true.

And I want that for you too. I don't want you to have to worry about money *ever again*.

So I got to work.

Now, hacking a proven system and using it for another purpose is one thing, but what if that system was *already* designed for who you are and how you are, right now with your own money?

I had been kicking these questions around, apparently, for a long time. Tommy's call was the sign I needed to prove my personal finance version of Profit First worked for people who have an hourly or seasonal income. Would the system work for people who are making ends meet on a fixed income while dealing with increasing inflation and economic uncertainty? With Travis's help, we started working with a test group of twenty-five A1 Garage Door Service employees from the Dream Manager program, in a Money Habit group. I called it the Money Habit system, not because we need to create all new habits, but because to be financially independent, we must work with the habits we *already have*.

Within just a few weeks, that Money Habit group experienced remarkable transformation. They paid off thousands of dollars in debt. They saved thousands for future expenses, for down payments on homes, for new cars, and for their kids' futures.

And within *six* months, they collectively saved a total of $282,830 and paid off $210,905 in debt. That's twenty-five people gaining nearly half a million dollars. In six months.

More importantly, they gained what I call "cash confidence." Like the entrepreneurs I'd been working with for nearly twenty years, these salaried, hourly-wage, and seasonal employees were confident they'd never have to worry about money again. Not that money challenges would never happen. They will. But now this group has a system that puts people in immediate control of any financial situation.

My team and I went on to implement the system with employees at other businesses in different industries and in different regions with varied costs of living and different types of earnings (salaried, hourly, seasonal, freelance, or gig work). That's when I knew for sure that the cash management system I created, the same system that saved hundreds of thousands of businesses from closing, could restore financial security for anyone who needed help, regardless of their life's path.

The Money Habit is for those of us who tried to follow the usual financial advice and petered out. If other approaches haven't worked for you, you are not at fault. They just don't suit you. So let me be bold: *This system might work for you specifically because those others have not.*

Using the Money Habit system doesn't require you to change who you are. You don't have to master a skill, use a software budgeting tool, or deprive yourself of everyday joys. Once you set it up, it will run automatically. You won't have to wonder whether you have enough money for this or that. You won't have to feel bad about your financial choices, including spending money on what you want. And you'll accumulate money to go after dreams you may have thought impossible, dreams you may have given up on long ago.

It was after Travis gave me the six-month numbers for the Money Habit program that he shared his comment about the American Dream. But that wasn't all he said.

"You know, you hear on the news that the American Dream is dead. No one can afford to buy a house. No one can go on vacation. But even in this tough economy, I'm seeing the people in the Money Habit program buy houses, go on vacations, save money for their kids' college. So I know it can be done."

Yes, Travis. It can be done.

Yes, you can do it. You don't have to be good at math, or have super willpower, or have perfect credit. You don't have to make a lot of money, or even have a predictable income. You don't have to understand personal finance.

You can do it.

The American Dream is not dead. It's yours for the taking.

1

You Have (Already) Won the Lottery

MY SON TYLER'S hand shook as he gave the check to his new wife, Cora.

Staring at the check, she said, "I've never seen this much money in my life."

Following the Money Habit system, my wife and I had set aside $50,000 for each of our three kids' weddings. And because Tyler and Cora had spent only $14,000 on their big day, we gave them a check for the balance in their wedding account ($36,000) to use however they saw fit. A rainy-day fund, a down payment on a home of their own, or toward some other dream.

Weeks later, I had to nudge Cora to deposit the check; she'd been holding on to it because she didn't know if her bank would accept a deposit of that size! She had never seen that much money, and I had never given that much. Ten years before that, I couldn't have written that check. We would have been able to give them a nice wedding gift, like a set of reasonably priced dishes or a pasta maker. But to pay for the wedding? To the tune of $50K? We couldn't have imagined ever being in that position to help our kids in that way, unless we won the lottery.

After I convinced Cora to deposit the check, it hit me: We *had* won the lottery.

And you have too.

You just may not know it yet.

People dream of getting checks with lots of zeros. Some play the lottery hoping for the big payout. Others eye old, ailing Uncle Richie Rich and his gracious will. Why? Because they want to be so financially secure that they never have to worry about money again, and they believe a windfall of cash will help them get there. Rightfully so.

Winning lotteries is a long shot. Better said, a *loooong* shot. But if you do have the rando-luck of a win, the most common jackpot amounts fall between $1 million and $3 million, often doled out through state lotteries or the more frequent secondary prizes. The odds of your million-dollar-plus win? One in about 12.5 million tries. Those odds suck.

To make the odds more understandable, if you played the lottery every day of the year for about 23,942 years (that is not a typo) you have a 50 percent chance of winning. With a minimum bet of $2 each time, you would pay $730 a year. And over those 24,000 years, you would pay $17.5 million to "win" maybe $2 million. In other words, lotteries drain you, your bank account, and your will to live. Don't play them. Hoping Uncle Richie Rich willed all his money to you instead of the twenty-five-year-old he recently "fell in love with" is far more likely to pay out but is mostly out of your control.

You don't have to make bets with impossible odds or pin your hopes on someone else's decisions, because you've already won. Seriously.

Let me explain. What if you won $2 million in today's lottery? Now, *that's* a good day. The lottery commission then gives you two options: You receive the funds in monthly installments over thirty years or you can cash out right away and get a lump sum of $1 million. Let's say you choose option one, since installments ensure you don't blow all that money on a spender-bender.

Now, what if I told you that you have already won exactly this amount of money? Probably more. And you have (wisely) chosen an installment plan that puts guardrails around your spending.

The average American and European earns roughly $2 million in salary over their lifetime. So your primary concern should not be how to come into more money today; it should be how to manage the money you are already coming into *more effectively* starting today.

You've probably heard that most lottery winners lose the money they won within a few years and end up more unhappy than they were when they "didn't have money." Case in point, the infamous story of Jack Whittaker, who won more than $300 million in the Powerball, circulates endlessly. What began as the "happiest day of his life" spiraled into lawsuits, a gambling addiction, the loss of family members to drug abuse, the loss of his uninsured home in a fire, and complete financial ruin. He is, however, the exception.

What you might not know is that the theory of lottery wins making you miserable has been debunked. It turns out lottery winners are pretty happy *when they manage their winnings wisely*. This insight explains the Whittaker case. Despite already being a multimillionaire before his record-breaking lottery win, he wasn't miserable because of the money; his mismanagement of it did him in. Shortly after his win, he bought a Lamborghini and did laps through his neighborhood, tossing money out the window. Not long after, thieves stole more than $500,000 in cash from him, which he had inexplicably stored in a silver suitcase in his car while he was inside a strip club. When asked why he made such reckless choices, his response was, "Because I can."

Financial success isn't about what you can do; it's about what you should do.

That brings me back to gifting the money to our son and his new wife. You might assume that the $50,000 we saved for our kids' weddings was possible because of how much money I earned. That's only part of the story. The real reason we were able to set aside that money was because I created a system that helped me manage my income and save for their weddings automatically over fifteen years. The system assigned a purpose to every dollar, ensuring all aspects of life, including Tyler and Cora's wedding, were accounted for. The Money Habit guided me on what I *should* do and, most importantly, it did the discipline part for me!

The odds on lotteries are heinous. But the odds on weddings are pretty darn good. They are likely to happen if you have kids, and there is a typical age range in which they will marry, so I play those odds. And when it comes to money management, playing the odds of life's probabilities will greatly help you too.

The Money Habit Formation

No matter your income, whether it's $200, $2,000, $20,000, $200,000, or $2 million, the system you are about to learn captures your cash flow and channels the money for you. Any financial outcome can be achieved by addressing three ingredients: amount, frequency, and time.

Amount × Frequency	= Challenge	Habit Forming	Time to Goal
Small × Infrequent	= Manageable but Inconsistent	Moderate	Slow
Large × Frequent	= Overwhelming but Consistent	Low	Fast
Large × Infrequent	= Overwhelming and Inconsistent	Very Low	Slowest
Small × Frequent	= Manageable and Consistent	Very High	Fastest

The Money Habit Formation Grid. Big deposits burn you out. Infrequent ones don't stick. But small, frequent allocations? They lock in the money habit fast. Your brain rewires with easy wins and rapid reps, and you hit goals faster than any other way.

Technically, I could save $50,000 if I put away just $1 (amount) per year (frequency) for 50,000 years (time to goal). Absurd, I know. But understanding these three factors allows you to wrap your head around what you want to do, what you can do, and how to adjust when you aren't happy with the progress.

Ramping Up Frequency

You can increase the frequency of your savings to reach your goal faster. For example, if I put away $1 (amount) every hour (frequency), I could save $50,000 in about five years and nine months (time to goal). If I increase the frequency even more, saving $1 every minute, then that fifty grand happens in just over one month.

Ramping Up Amount

You can also increase the amount you save each time. For example, if I put away $100 (amount) per month (frequency), I would reach $50,000 in just over forty-one years. If I double the amount to $200 per month, I cut that time in half to just over twenty years.

Combining Frequency and Amount

The real magic happens when you ramp up both the amount and frequency. For example, if I save $25 (amount) every day (frequency), I could hit $50,000 in about five years and six months. And if I push my savings to $100 every day, I could achieve the same goal in just one year and four months.

This approach aligns with cognitive load theory, which suggests that smaller, more frequent actions are easier for our brains to process and sustain over time. When a goal feels manageable, like saving $25 each day, we're less likely to feel overwhelmed

compared to larger, less frequent amounts like $760 per month.*
Even though they work out to be the same amount.

By breaking savings into bite-sized, consistent steps, you reduce mental strain and increase the likelihood of sticking to the plan. As you establish your Money Habit, you will hear my constant drum beat to allocate funds weekly or biweekly. It is how you stack small financial building blocks sequentially, resulting in substantial money gains without substantial effort.

Now that you understand how amount and frequency interact with time, you can take control of your financial goals. By adjusting just one, or better, both factors, you can achieve outcomes that might seem impossible at first glance.

It is the money system, not the money I earn, that has given me the ability to handle almost anything life throws at me and keeps me worry-free about how I'm going to pay for it. Isn't that why we all want a windfall of cash? To do what we want, when we want, worry-free, forever?

When Life Expects Us to Pay Up

Within minutes of getting the call that our daughter was in the hospital, my wife, Krista, had booked a flight out of Newark, New Jersey, for early the next morning and had already started packing. Adayla had fallen eighteen feet from a wall while rock climbing near her home in Tennessee.

Thankfully, she was okay, but she had snapped her ankle. Her foot had twisted completely. As she looked down, she realized she wasn't staring at the top of her foot, she was staring at the bottom. In that split-second, frozen in time, she thought, *I've never seen my sole before... so weird.* Then the pain hit like a streaking meteor, and she blacked out.

---

* $25 per day × 30.42 average days per month = $760.42. Rounded down, that's $760 a month.

I had been keeping our insurance costs down by using a "catastrophe" policy with a high deductible of $10,000. This catastrophe was surely about to make us pony up a big chunk of cash. And, we were soon to find out, that ten grand was a mere drop in the bucket.

After she arrived in Tennessee, Krista purchased some medical supplies for Adayla, including a scooter to help her get around once she was allowed to get out of bed. Krista also paid for all the meals and groceries for the two-and-a-half weeks she stayed with Adayla while she recovered from surgery. And, because I was traveling for speaking engagements during that stretch, we hired a house sitter to check in on our house, water plants, and bring in the mail, as well as a dog sitter to walk and feed Archer, our mutt. The bills started to add up.

Next-day flight:	$584
Deductible for surgery:	$10,000
Scooter:	$153
Medical supplies:	$91
Meals and groceries/2.5 weeks/two people:	$520
House sitter (two weeks for while I was away):	$350
Dog sitter (last-minute with overnight care): a whopping	$1,200
Total unexpected expenses:	**$12,898**

If the accident had happened a dozen years earlier, we would have been screwed. I would have been doing the mental math and freaking out about how we would cover the unexpected expenses, likely scrambling to pull together some combination of personal loans and credit cards. And then once we figured that out, we'd be freaking out about how we would eventually make those payments.

Worrying about money would have added to the concern we had for our daughter, making a tough situation a full-blown crisis. You can't adequately attend to an emergency when there is a constant undercurrent of a *financial* emergency. Adding insult to injury, at least for me, money worries come out in anger and frustration. I would be snippy at best, a jerky jerk at worst.

Except none of that happened. Krista wasn't worried. I wasn't worried. We knew we had enough cash to cover everything in our HEALTH savings account. And because we had the cash, we could act quickly so Krista could be right by Adayla's side as soon as possible.

Sitting in my hotel room the day after Krista arrived in Tennessee, I called her for an update. All was well. Our daughter was in pain, but the surgery went smoothly and with the help of physical therapy, she'd get full use of her ankle again within a year. After I hung up the phone, I sat quietly in my room and thought about how different our lives were since the dark days of when we were drowning in debt. Back then, I dreamed of being free from the financial roller coaster, and I worked tirelessly to change it, but I couldn't get a handle on it.

Until my daughter, that same young woman who had just broken her ankle, saved my life.

The Piggy Bank

By the time I was thirty-five, I had built and sold two multimillion-dollar companies. Before you start picturing private jets, yachts, and Lambos (with me throwing money out the window), let me stop you right there. These companies were far from financially fit, and truth be told, neither was I. The difference between what a business makes and what its owner actually takes home is massive. The buyers bought my businesses for strategic reasons, not because I made these companies into money-making machines. That's what the new owners planned to do with their acquisitions.

Alas, the truth of the situation was something I couldn't see. I thought I was a rich mofo. Two company exits meant a couple of years of take-home income in the chunky six figures. I was able to grow 'em and get out of 'em before they crumbled.

I was the master of the pump and dump. You know, where you build up something fast with little to no structural integrity (a house of cards) and sell it off before it all comes tumbling down. My biggest pump and dump? My ego. I pumped up a big fat ego and dumped my common sense. With my "obvious" Midas touch I decided to become an angel investor. Spoiler alert: I was a disaster. I didn't lose "just a little" money; in less than two years, I lost every penny I got from the "lottery-win" sales of my businesses. All of it.

Things spiraled fast. Bills piled up. I stopped opening them. Unknown numbers? Straight to voicemail. Debt consolidation companies hounded me with multiple calls a day, and their bright, shame-inducing envelopes stuffed my mailbox weekly. My financial mess wasn't just private anymore; it had gone public. And it was humiliating.

I did everything I could to keep it hidden. Every day, I'd rush to the mailbox before Krista could get to it, shoving those ugly reminders of my failure deep into a drawer. I told myself it was to protect her, to keep her from worrying. But the truth? I didn't want her to know just how bad it had gotten. I didn't want her to see me for what I felt I had become: a financial disaster who had run out of money, out of luck, and nearly out of hope.

I started to fixate on who would find out I had gotten us into a financial mess. Could the neighbors see my slumped shoulders and sagging head from their front window when I opened my mailbox? Had they received any of the collection notices by accident? What did the mail carrier think? I was so embarrassed. By this point I was sending numbers that I *did* know to voicemail. My withdrawal was the start of a depression.

In his classic book *Walden*, Henry David Thoreau wrote, "The mass of men lead lives of quiet desperation." That sums up my life during those dark days. I was desperate to get us out from under debt and off the financial roller-coaster ride, without anyone noticing a thing.

Desperate people do desperate things. So I tried anything and everything: "get rich quick" books, the law of attraction and all that manifesting stuff—I even tried playing the lottery. I wondered if that sign on telephone poles that read "Stuff envelopes at home. Earn $1,000/week" might be legit. (It's not.) I wanted ways to be financially sound so badly, I started to convince myself that obvious scams were the real deal. See what I mean? Desperate. I knew, deep down inside, that none of these "strategies" would work. But we'll do (and believe) all sorts of weird stuff when we don't have other options.

I also reverted to the fabled "money shuffle." I moved money from here to cover a cost over there, and then I took from there to cover something else over here. I kept moving money around, trying to keep us afloat, until one day there was nothing left to move around. It all went down on the day meant for hearts, roses, and chocolate.

On Valentine's Day 2008, my accountant called. "Good news, Mike. I got a jump-start on your taxes this year and just finished your return for 2007. You owe only twenty-eight thousand dollars." This was the last tax bill associated with the sale of company two. Money that was totally gone twelve or so months prior.

Good news? Hardly. I had $10,000 in a mix of accounts and between the tax bill, the accountant's bill, living expenses, and the growing monthly minimum of credit cards, I'd need four times that amount. Where would I find the money?

In the greatest of ironies, that day I came home with a hopeless heart because for our family, Valentine's Day was a special deal. At dinner, we would exchange cards and stories about what we loved about each other. It was one of my favorite days of the year, yet I opened the door filled with dread.

I would have to come clean. It was time to tell my family the truth about our finances.

At dinner, Krista and the kids could see something was up. When she asked if I was okay, I started crying. I was so full of shame. I mean, I was (supposedly) the breadwinner, the guy who provided for the family, yet I couldn't do my one friggin' job.

Finally I said, "I lost everything. Every single penny."

Tyler and our youngest son, Jake, sat motionless. Stunned. Frozen.

Adayla was nine at the time. Her eyes big and her shoulders tense, she looked terrified. I don't know if it was because her daddy was sobbing, or she comprehended what I had done, or both. She jumped up from the table and ran as fast as she could. On those spindly legs of hers, she booked up the stairs into her room and slammed the door shut.

You and I have made a commitment to be providers. That is why you are reading this book after all. You have committed to provide for yourself. You may have committed to provide for your family. You may be providing for parents, kids, relatives, others. The thing is, providing financial security is a form of protection. But I was such a failure that I couldn't protect my own family. I wanted to run away from the circumstances that I had brought down upon us. So, to see my daughter run away from me was brutally painful. At the same time, I got it. She was doing exactly what I wanted to do.

Except she wasn't running away from me. She was running to her bedroom to save me.

Behind the closed door, she grabbed her most prized possession and then flung the door open. That little nine-year-old girl raced back down the steps with her piggy bank, the one she had received as a gift when she was born. I had told her that dreams come true when you manage your money well. (I am aware of the extraordinary hypocrisy as I write this.)

Dutiful, she had been saving nickels, dimes, and dollars for the horse she wanted to have one day. The rubber stopper on her piggy bank had been secured with masking tape, duct tape, and rubber bands so "a robber wouldn't steal it."

She handed me her piggy bank and then, in her tiny, nine-year-old voice, said, "Stop crying, Daddy. We're going to make it."

Telling my family we had no money left was my rock-bottom moment. At least that's what I thought. There's a saying about rock-bottom moments, and you probably know it: "As difficult as it is at the bottom, at least there's only one way to go... up." It's a beautiful sentiment. Too bad it's total bullshit.

The reality is, when you hit rock bottom, life drags you along the ground. Shards of self-disdain slice your skin, grains of loathing grind your eyes, and boulders of hopelessness crush your bones. If you know, you know.

I had always said if I couldn't provide for my family through a business of my own, I would get a job working anywhere, doing anything. If McDonald's was hiring, I would take it. If UPS needed a night shift fella to move boxes, I was in. At least so I said. When I hit that lower-than-low point, I didn't stay true to my word. Instead, I borrowed money from soon-to-be-maxed-out credit cards and lines of credit, from friends and family, all to "keep the business going." And I drank a lot. I drank to feel less ashamed. To feel less, period.

For me, rock bottom became two years of (self-diagnosed) functional depression. While Adayla's confident declaration had momentarily filled me with hope that we would make it, I had no idea *how* we would make it. How *I* would make it. And that's when the depression started. I tried several tools to lift it. I started a daily success diary, which did nothing. I joined a men's group, which helped some of the time, but most of the time being in the presence of guys who were financially strong, or at least seemed that way, only amplified my shame.

The only thing that would work to get me off the ground and return me to a peaceful state of mind was financial stability.

More Money Is Not (Always) the Answer

Eventually, the cash games stop and reality hits. This didn't happen when I drained my own accounts. It happened when I couldn't spend anyone else's cash either, because I had borrowed everything I could.

That was the first time I took a hard, honest look at how I had run my businesses, and I noticed a pattern: I was obsessed with having more (getting more money) and had spent almost no time learning how to manage what I already had (controlling money more). I chased that lottery-level windfall; I did not build wealth.

For people who are living in poverty, who can't pull themselves up by their bootstraps because they don't even have boots, more money coming in *is* the answer to their immediate problems. But for the rest of us, more money will help us only so much before we end up back in the same hellhole. This is because we keep trying to implement budgets and financial strategies that go against our natural habits. And that's when we tend to go haywire.

Bank Balance Budgeting

It's payday! You look at your bank balance and suddenly, after a week of eating leftovers, you're flush. So you start spending. Dinner and a movie. A purchase at your favorite store. A gift for a friend. Then, come Monday, you realize you have to pay the phone bill, and you owe your coworker Jan for the lunch she covered the other week. Don't forget about the student loan payment you have on auto-pay. Your payment for that roof over your head is due in thirteen days and you're wondering, yet again, if you might be short.

"Bank balance budgeting" is making spending decisions based solely on the number you see in your account, rather than accounting for upcoming bills and automatic payments. This approach leads to recurring financial stress.

So we decide it's time to "stick to a budget." And that works just about as well as you'd expect.

Here's how I used to run my business and personal finances: I'd set a budget at the start of the year, and then within a month or two, I would have blown it due to "unforeseen circumstances." An unexpected expense, something we wanted to buy or something we needed to buy, would come up. And another one. And then another one. This is not uncommon. According to *U.S. News & World Report*, 80 percent of New Year's resolutions fail by the second week of February. We're terrible at sticking with new habits.

With my budget merely a suggestion, I'd resort to my tendency to check our bank balance to see if we had enough money right now to cover whatever we had to cover "right now."

If the checking account seemed to have a healthy balance, we'd spend. Except that balance had to cover a lot of other things. Maybe some payments hadn't cleared yet, or an automatic withdrawal would surprise me yet again. Maybe an annual expense was coming up and we hadn't accounted for it. Did we really have enough money, or not?

What appeared to be a healthy balance on payday would lull me into a false sense of security. Then, a few days or weeks later, I'd look at the low or negative balance and wonder where all the money went. Then the overdraft charge would crush my bones.

I'd think, *Maybe I just need a different budget. Maybe I'm doing it wrong.*

We turn to financial experts who tell us to budget, and we try that. But budgets work about as well as diets, which fail in the long term 95 percent of the time. Ninety-five percent! That means pretty much every diet will fail eventually. Notice how I didn't say, "Every dieter will fail." It's not us. It really isn't.

Except we think it is our fault. We *believe* it is our fault.

Maybe I need therapy. Maybe I need to figure out why I overspend.

Therapy is helpful, and mental health is vital, for sure. *And* the solution may be simpler and faster than uncovering our emotional issues around money.

The late Howard Farkas was a renowned psychologist known for his unprecedented success helping his clients recover from chronic binge eating and emotional eating. In his book, *8 Keys to End Emotional Eating,* Farkas explains the underlying reason it's so hard for people to stay on a diet and stop eating food they know they probably shouldn't eat is that there is an internal conflict between control and autonomy. He says an aspect of emotional eating is the "transgressive motive," a "taboo-breaking thrill of defying the rules."

Farkas writes, "There's a conscious part that you think of as your real self. It's compliant, eager to please, and wants to do the right thing, including diet and exercise, and generally go along with social expectations. There's also a part that you're probably not aware of that's more rebellious. It instinctively reacts against restrictions on your freedom, including the freedom to choose what to eat. These are the two sides of the struggle that results in emotional eating, and this conflict must be understood to be resolved."

So basically, we *want* to budget, but we also want our freedom. We rebel sometimes out of necessity, and sometimes just because we wanna. This is why willpower doesn't work long term. We are wired for the need to comply to social norms (don't go broke) but we also want to break free from those social norms (buy this fun toy).

What does it look like when budgeting starts to fail? When we want to buy something outside of our budget, we check the good ol' bank balance again. It seems like we have plenty of money. Shouldn't be a problem. We can just shift something around later, right? Now the budget, like diets and New Years' resolutions, is blown, and we start to feel pretty bad about our choices. Why can't we get it together like Jan in marketing (who we *still* owe ten bucks for lunch)?

Let's not torture ourselves anymore, okay? It's not you. You're not a bad person, or bad with money, or unable to kick your bad habits. Our inability to stick to a budget is not our fault. It's how we're wired. All of us, as in humans. We just don't want to be restricted all the time.

Farkas says the solution is to bring these two parts of us, control and autonomy, into balance. When I read about that in his book, I got chills. Because there's that word again. Balance.

How do we restore balance between our two natural tendencies, so we don't feel the need to rebel and screw up our finances? We allow ourselves to spend what we want in our *bank balance*. We keep doing what we've already been doing: checking the bank to see if we have money and spending based on what's there.

We don't *stop* bank balance budgeting. We make it work for us.

We set up a system (control) so our inner rebel can live (autonomy).

That is the fundamental difference in the Money Habit system, the difference that beats those crappy New Year's resolution and diet statistics and helps you create permanent change. I'll show you exactly how to do it in the next chapter.

How I Figured It Out

In my low, low, lower-than-low rock-bottom place, dodging bill collectors, it finally dawned on me: *What if I stop trying to use systems that require me to have discipline or to change who I am? What if I had a money system that works with what I already do? What if I figure out how to manage my finances by doing what I am already doing multiple times a day: looking at my bank account?*

That's when I came up with the Profit First system for my business. Even in my mental state, I knew that, as a business owner, I needed to get my business finances in order first. If I could consistently be profitable, the proceeds would be my source of income. In a nutshell, Profit First involves transferring a percentage of income into different bank accounts (envelopes) that are earmarked for specific purposes. Using Profit First, my business went from being a money pit to a profitable, money-making machine in just a few months. I'm generally an optimistic guy, but even I was shocked at how fast it worked!

I then went on to build three more multimillion-dollar businesses, this time with sound cash management in place. As in businesses that actually pay the owner and all their employees a real salary.

Profit First worked so well for my business that I immediately started using it with my family's personal finances. I adjusted the percentages to account for different goals and circumstances. I kept tweaking it for personal finances until I was sure it would work for anyone. For people who have a job, people who are paid by the hour or who receive a salary, people who run a business or a side hustle, people who are doing okay financially but want to do better, and people who are crawling back from that dark place and haven't yet seen the light at the end of the tunnel.

I call it the Money Habit system and it works because it uses the habits you already have. You don't have to be disciplined or good at math, or to understand financial jargon. You don't have to spend years learning finance or bookkeeping. And you don't have to change who you are. Because let's face it, if becoming worry-free requires me and you to change who we naturally are, we'll be stuck on the roller-coaster ride forever.

When Adayla said, "Daddy, we're going to make it," I was humbled by her sacrifice, but dismissed it as a child's ignorance about what we were facing. But maybe ignorance wasn't the right thought. It was innocence. I couldn't believe it possible. I was too low, and too mired in the way that you are "supposed to" manage money. Yet she was right.

We did make it. Within a year of my personal finances being in control, the debt consolidation notices stopped coming and the debt collectors stopped calling. We had a small emergency fund and enough money to pay our bills on time every month, and we had started setting aside money for the stuff we wanted and the dreams I thought we'd have to leave behind.

We made it, not because I figured out how to make more money (inherent to an entrepreneur's income is volatility), or because I got really good at budgeting (I'm not). We made it because I finally had a system that worked. A system that didn't demand I become someone I'm not. I could stay myself (minus the massive ego), and the system would still deliver. A system that was so rock solid that it worked, even if I—ahem—cheated a bit.

Cash Confidence Is Power

A couple of months into Adayla's recovery from ankle surgery, she received a notice from the insurance company that they would not cover any of the hospital bill. Neatly folded in with the notice was the statement "Patient Responsibility: $75,000." Adayla panicked. She now had to pay a bill that would bury her. She called Krista, crying, exasperated, panicked she'd have to work two or three jobs for years to cover it. She was frozen, unable to think of how to get out from under the bill. I too was stunned momentarily, but I knew what to do next.

I immediately called our agent, Dan Ritter, and we started the complex process of challenging the insurance's denial. Still, Adayla was convinced she'd have to pay the bill. And from my understanding, we were in for a dog fight with the insurance company based on a technicality they used to skirt responsibility. So, yeah, that monster bill was going to be on my daughter's lap.

"Let's consider the worst-case scenario," I said. "If the worst happens and insurance doesn't pay, we have enough money in our emergency account to pay for it in full. Don't worry, Adayla. We can cover it."

Don't worry, Adayla. We can cover it.

To comfort my daughter fifteen years after she offered up her piggy bank to me was a full-circle moment I'll never forget. I still get choked up thinking about it. Adayla, in her nine-year-old mind, was confident we would be okay because she had "cash confidence," her piggy bank with the duct-taped stopper. Now I was able to pull from our savings, if needed, to cover her outrageous medical bill, because *I had cash confidence.* My wife and I had squirreled away money monthly into our emergency account and had $100,000, more than enough to cover the bill.

Once she understood that we could pay the bill if we had to, Adayla felt comfort. Her focus shifted from fear and anger to working on a path forward. When we are overwhelmed by financial anxieties, it's freaking hard to see a way out of it. And it's damn near impossible to fight for what's rightfully yours. With the newfound cash confidence, we started making calls and gathering documentation. Six months of a pragmatic, persistent approach tipped the scales in her favor, and eventually the insurance company agreed to cover 90 percent of Adayla's hospital bill. Thanks to Dan for the guidance. Thanks to our emergency fund for the confidence.

When you know you have enough money to cover everything you need, that's "cash confidence." And with the help of this book, you're about to get it.

The $36,000 Check

Since setting up the Money Habit system in my own life, Krista and I bought our dream home. We intend to pay off our thirty-year mortgage in less than twelve years. We paid for all three of our kids' college educations in full. We set aside money for retirement and emergencies of every kind. We have individual slush funds, which allows me to go to a Virginia Tech football weekend with the guys, guilt free (Go, Hokies!), and Krista to go on a girls' trip to Napa Valley, guilt free (Go, cab francs!). And the best part, we have had a ton of fun together on adventures and trips all over the world. Cash confidence has given us access to our dream life. I intend to do the same for you.

These outcomes—no debt, early mortgage payoffs, trips, healthy emergency funds, college funds, and even wedding funds—may seem impossible to you right now. You may wonder if a system as simple as transferring funds to separate bank accounts can really make all this happen. Yes, it can.

You may think the Money Habit system won't work for you because you have too much debt, or you don't earn enough, or you aren't good with numbers. I didn't believe it would work for me either. But it has more than worked. It has transformed my life. And it has transformed the lives of at least a million others. You'll hear some of their stories in this book.

Yes, The Money Habit will work for you. It's not complicated to set up, and once that's done, the system runs automatically. You simply need to take the first step and decide to give it a try.

You don't have to be stuck in the ups and downs of the financial roller-coaster ride. You don't have to be at the mercy of inflation or worry that you won't have enough money to cover the things that are important to you and your family. You don't have to stay in that place where one disaster, one accident, one catastrophe could bury you in debt for years or for life. You *will* have the cash confidence to live the life you dream about.

Congrats, lottery winner, your financial freedom starts now.

2

The Money Habit System

STOP RIGHT HERE. If you're not ready to step up and do the thing that will forever fix your wallet, put this book down and go back to hoping your finances magically fix themselves.

Yes, you read that right. I've never started a chapter like this before, and admittedly, asking you to put down my book may not be a smart idea. But it had to be done. Your financial future depends on it. And your finances are far more important than me selling a book.

The biggest barrier to financial freedom is not a lack of knowledge; it is in not doing what you know you need to do. So, you can't skim. You can't get to this "when you have the time." This chapter is the game changer, and if you don't act on it, you won't get results.

Just give me one hour. That's all I ask. With all the love in the world, I implore you: Buckle up, Buttercup, and do this shit. We good? Good. Then, I have one final plea, I promise. This chapter will give you the basic overview of the Money Habit system, but to really understand it, you've got to *do it*. You've got to experience it. And I want you to do it today, even if it is ten o'clock at night, and you're comfortably tucked in bed in your favorite pj's. Money mastery is a $24 \times 7 \times 365$ thing. Start now.

Not "tomorrow."
Not "soon."
Today.
Even if you are sitting there in your undies.
Let's get to work.

Use Multiple Bank Accounts

Every summer, we take a family vacation to Long Beach Island. One morning several years ago, before I perfected the Money Habit system, we were out to brunch at one of our favorite restaurants, Uncle Will's, and there was a guy at the table next to us who struck up a conversation, I think, because I was wearing a Virginia Tech hat.

I felt extra generous. So as a surprise, I told the waiter, "Hey, don't tell that guy, but I want to cover his meal."

The check came, I yanked out my trusty credit card, and the waiter smiled. "Sir, we've gone cash only."

I froze. I looked at the debit card nestled in my wallet and at the bank machine in the corner that the waiter kindly pointed out to me. Did I have enough in that account to cover the bill? I had no clue. And since I didn't even have enough cash on hand to cover my meal, let alone his, I had to turn to my sister, her husband, my niece, and my son to scramble together enough money to pay for this guy's meal.

It wasn't even that I didn't have the money. I paid everyone back right away. The real problem? I had no awareness of my finances. I didn't know what was available, and I wasn't tracking what I could actually spend.

That's the difference now. With the Money Habit system, I never have to wonder. And I definitely don't have to do the I'll-pay-you-back-later-I-swear scramble for cash ever again.

In the introduction, I talked about the envelope system that's been around for ages. You designate envelopes for different expenses, like rent, "mad money," and groceries, and then stash your cash in the envelopes. When you need to run to the store for groceries, you use only the money in the corresponding envelope. Seems simple enough, right? Except there's a couple of problems with the envelope system. What's stopping you from shifting money from one envelope to another? Nothing. It's too easy to pull money out of your "someday" envelopes: the ones labeled Rainy Day, Down Payment for Dream Home, and Summer Vacation. You think you'll replace the money, but you rarely do.

The solution is to open multiple bank accounts for specific expenditures and transfer a portion of your income to each account. And to keep you from borrowing from one "envelope" to cover an unexpected expense or a spending spree, you'll open a couple of accounts at different financial institutions so you cannot easily transfer funds between accounts. You can keep your "bank balance budgeting" habit and let your inner rebel be free. This freedom is not a "bad" habit at all. In fact, it will save the day.

Here are the six foundational accounts I want you to set up:

1 **INCOME:** This is where your total earnings are deposited. You will never pay bills from this account. Instead, you will disburse funds to the other accounts from this account. You will not get a debit card for this account, because you won't use it to buy anything.

2 **NEEDS:** This is an account for essential expenses necessary for daily living, such as your housing payment, car insurance, groceries, and utilities. You will get a debit card for this account because you will need it for your everyday needs.

3 **WANTS:** This is your discretionary spending account for things you want but can live without, such as entertainment, dining out, or new clothes. You will get a debit card for this account. You can choose a different card design or label the cards with the account names to easily identify which debit card to use in which circumstances.

4. **DREAMS:** This account is to save for aspirational spending for major life goals tied to personal fulfillment, such as vacations, investments, or achievements. This money is sacred, so keep it out of sight and out of mind (and at a different bank) to avoid dipping into it for everyday wants. When you're finally ready to make that big buy, you'll transfer a portion of this money into your WANTS account to spend with intention and celebration.

5. **FIX/FUTURE:** Use this account to eliminate debt and secure your financial future. While you have debt, it's your FIX account. Once debt-free, rename it FUTURE and use it to build long-term savings. Don't get a debit card for this account. Set up auto-payments from it to crush debt consistently. When you shift to FUTURE, use automatic transfers to investment accounts or other forms of a "security stash" to keep momentum and never miss a deposit.

6. **EMERGENCY:** This account is savings for unforeseen expenses, such as medical emergencies or urgent home or car repairs. Minimally, you will set this up as a hidden account at your current bank to crush the temptation of using it for anything that isn't an emergency. To make it truly seem out of reach, set it up at a different financial institution. When you do need it, transfer the funds to the NEEDS account and pay for that emergency.

You may be thinking, *This dude is out of his mind. How am I supposed to keep track of so many accounts? What's my bank going to say?* I get it. And I know six bank accounts may seem like a lot at first, but really, the pain is over once you set them up. And your banker? They'll be thrilled about how much moola you're moving through their bank.

In chapter 3, I will give you a handy-dandy chart, called The Money Target, that will help you figure out your disbursement percentages: how much to transfer from your INCOME account into the other five accounts.

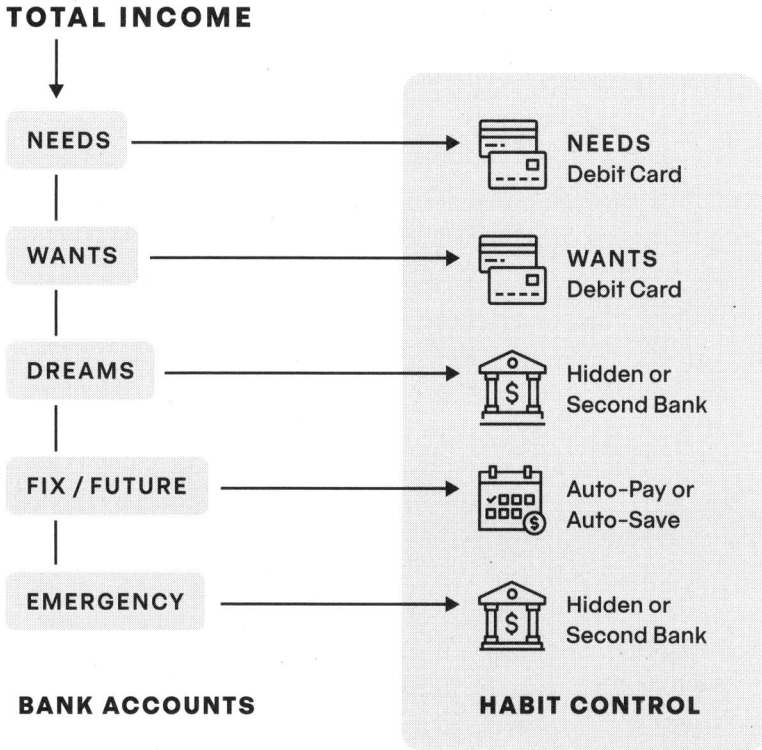

The Money Habit System. Rather than ask you to fight your existing habits, the Money Habit system channels them. Your total household income hits the INCOME account, then a percentage (or fixed dollar amount) flows into NEEDS, WANTS, DREAMS, FIX/FUTURE, and EMERGENCY to give you instant clarity on what money is for what purpose. Debit cards control daily spending in the NEEDS and WANTS accounts. Hard-to-access accounts, which are hidden or at a second bank, protect long-term funds. Automated payments knock down debt. Automated transfers build savings.

Why Fix and Future Are the Same Account

You may be wondering why the FIX account (for debt reduction) and the FUTURE account (for savings accumulation) aren't separate. Simple: Having both accounts at the same time messes with your behavioral wiring and gives you too much leeway to drift off course. When FIX and FUTURE run side by side, it weakens habit formation and makes it easier to justify poor decisions, like carrying debt while believing you're building a strong financial future.

The Money Habit system is built around financial seasons (you'll learn more about those in chapter 3). At specific times, your main job is to fix debt. No splitting attention between past mistakes and future goals. When your account is labeled FIX *or* FUTURE, never both, every time you log into your bank, you instantly know your top priority. That kind of insight builds momentum.

Behavioral psychology backs this up: in particular, attentional bias. We focus most on what's right in front of us. So, if you see FUTURE money sitting next to FIX debt, your brain gets confused. You lose urgency. You rationalize. You slip.

One account, one purpose: That's how you build the habit and keep it strong. And when the debt is gone and your FIX account becomes your FUTURE account, that shift isn't just a renaming, it's a milestone. You've earned it. Just don't go back. Debt is common, but that does *not* mean it's normal. Kill it first. Then move forward, permanently.

Remove Temptation

As I mentioned earlier, we tend to "borrow" from accounts we've set up for a specific purpose, usually to handle unexpected expenses or buy something we *just have to have*. Instead of trying to change that habit, we're going to put guardrails around it.

The funds for your INCOME, NEEDS, and WANTS accounts will stay visible at your primary bank, but your DREAMS and EMERGENCY accounts will live elsewhere. Or at the very least, be well hidden from the most likely thief: you. Out of sight really is out of mind, and that's exactly where you need some of your money to be.

Again, your FIX/FUTURE account will be set to auto-pay (debt) or auto-save (investments), so the money moves on to do its work before you can get your sticky fingers on it. Because if you "borrow" from those funds, it's not borrowing. It's stealing from yourself. And every time you do it, you chip away at the effectiveness of the entire system.

This is usually where people ask me, "Why not just move money straight from INCOME to pay off the credit card or invest?" Fair question. But that "extra" step of sending money to FIX or FUTURE first isn't busywork. It's a behavioral firewall. It makes you see the money, feel the decision, and own the move. Skip that, and the cash just disappears. The FIX and FUTURE accounts act as staging areas. You spot the amount, confirm the action, and in that brief pause, you reinforce your money habit. Visibility builds accountability. And accountability makes good behavior stick.

If you participate in your company's 401(k) program or health insurance savings program, you're already doing this. The funds are deducted from your paycheck before you get it, so you don't have access to that money and you don't have to worry about spending it or covering those expenses. The money is subsequently stored at a bank or financial institution other than your regular bank. Better still, your investment account likely prohibits access without a penalty, until you reach a certain age. Pull the funds out earlier than the designated date and you may pay a penalty. Temptation removed!

Establish a Rhythm

When we don't have a handle on our bills and available cash, it causes worry. This is why it's important to establish a rhythm of disbursing funds from INCOME to your NEEDS, WANTS, DREAMS, FIX/FUTURE, and EMERGENCY accounts.

You'll begin by test-driving the Money Habit system manually for two months. That means no automation yet. Every time you get paid, you'll log into your bank, look at INCOME, and intentionally transfer all your INCOME funds into your dedicated accounts, *then* you'll pay your bills from them. All of this is done by looking at your bank accounts. No spreadsheets, no bookkeeping system, no budget necessary. (As a reminder, in chapter 3 I'll give you the percentages you'll need to figure out how much of your income to disburse to each account.)

Over time, following this rhythm will give you a better sense of your personal cash flow. Like when you need to set aside more, if you need to change your rhythm, that sort of thing. You'll develop a kind of intuition about money that you haven't experienced yet.

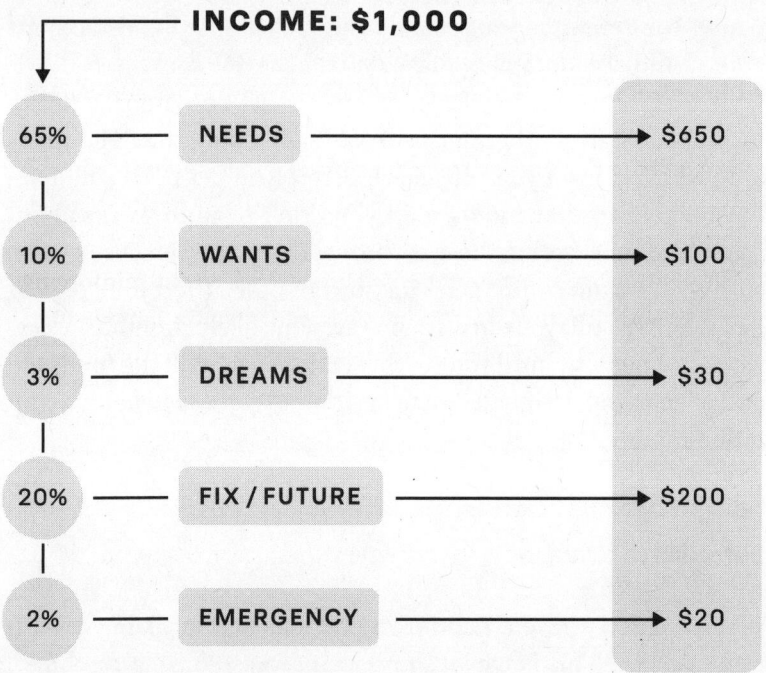

Example of Money Habit allocations. A $1,000 deposit lands in the INCOME account. On allocation day, funds flow out based on set percentages (or fixed amounts), so every dollar has a clear job before it's used. In this example, 65 percent ($650) goes to NEEDS, 10 percent to WANTS, and so on. One glance at your accounts tells you what's available for what purpose.

Yes, it takes a little effort at this stage, but there's a reason for this. Each transfer will give you a micro-win, a new awareness, and your first experience of control over your money.

After two months of doing this manually, you'll set up automatic transfers, so your system runs itself. This means your bank will handle the allocations for you. Based on the fixed dollar amount or percentages (some banks do both!) you assign, your bank will distribute the money from your INCOME account into your NEEDS, WANTS, and other accounts on a set schedule.

In his book *I Will Teach You to Be Rich*, my friend Ramit Sethi writes, "Sometimes the most advanced thing you can do is the basics, consistently." (I completely agree.) Ramit is a big advocate of automation. By setting up auto-transfers into his savings and investment accounts, each part of his financial system works together, seamlessly. Having his finances on autopilot gives him a cascade of benefits, among them: His money accumulates while he sleeps, and he doesn't worry about covering bills or having enough money to retire one day.

Automation isn't just about convenience; it's about reinforcing the habits and structure you've already put in place and understand. You'll know exactly where your money is going because you've been actively managing it for two months.

The One Account Challenge

The Money Habit system is your worry-free path to financial independence. But right now, you might not feel very worry free. Maybe you are waiting for your next paycheck before you can fill your gas tank. Maybe your house payment is coming due again and you are scrambling to make it work. Maybe it is worse.

Or maybe your frustration comes from not knowing when you can afford something you really want. When can you finally take that vacation you keep talking about? When will you be able to go out to dinner without putting it on the credit card again?

No matter the financial situation, we all have that one thing. Something that keeps us worrying or wondering. At the core, every financial consideration comes down to the same two questions.

When will I be able to cover that expense?
When will I be able to afford that thing?

The Money Habit answers these questions no matter where you are financially. But still, one thing can get in the way: feeling overwhelmed.

Some people find the idea of opening all these accounts at once too much. Like walking into a packed restaurant where everyone is talking at the same time, too many accounts can make too much noise, at first. If that sounds like you, before we run the risk of too many voices coming at you, we are going to start small. Just one financial conversation between you and a bank account. *The one conversation that will help you stop worrying or wondering.*

Just like with any good habit, the way to build it to the highest level is to start small before doing it all. So start by opening just one new bank account designated for either something you're worried about covering or something you really want to purchase.

So here's your mission, should you choose to accept it:

1 Determine what the account will be for. Ask yourself which financial stressor is on your mind most often. Do you worry about covering rent each month? Paying for groceries any given week? Affording your kids' summer camp registration? Or do you find yourself wondering when you can finally buy those new sneakers? Or something bigger, like a weekend getaway? If the question "When can I afford this?" keeps popping up or causes stress, that's your cue to set up an account for it.

2 Open just one new account at your bank and nickname it after your biggest financial stressor. When starting out, it's usually a NEED, but it could also be a WANT or DREAM. Choose a name that instantly clarifies its purpose. To keep things organized, precede the nickname with N (NEED), W (WANT), or D (DREAM) so you always know what the money is for, at a glance.

For example, N-Groceries, N-Rent, W-Dinner Out, D-Vacation, or D-A Gift for Mike.*

3 Allocate money to your new account every time you get paid. For essential expenses like rent or groceries, set aside a fixed dollar amount each week or per paycheck to ensure the expense is fully covered when needed. For example, if your rent is $1,600 per month, you might allocate $400 per week or $800 per biweekly paycheck to your N-Rent account. If it's an annual expense, like summer camp fees, divide the total by the number of weeks or pay periods until it's due, and set aside that amount to W-Summer Camp regularly. For expenses without a deadline, like dining out or vacations, allocate a small percentage of your income instead. These expenses are more flexible, so you can adjust as needed.

4 Use the funds in this dedicated account only for its exclusive purpose. Don't have enough money in it to buy the new shoes? Then your "when" hasn't happened yet, and you are not ready to buy the shoes. Don't have enough money to pay for all the groceries? Then you need to consider how much you spend on groceries *or* the possibility you are spending money on fancy shoes at the expense of your pantry.

When you complete the One Account Challenge, email me at mike@mikemichalowicz.com with the subject line "My Money Habit Starts Now!" so I can easily spot it in my inbox. There is no better accountability mechanism than telling me you're committed. I'll be sure to email you back; just be patient since I am traveling constantly and not always on top of my inbox.

---

* That last one is a joke. But believe it or not, some people have actually sent me checks. If this method has served you so deeply that you're tempted to do the same, please instead donate to the Community Service Society of New York (and tell me when you do). This organization helps people facing economic insecurity, and it quite literally saved my father from abject poverty when he was a child. Your contribution could do the same for someone else.

With this step complete, you have already handled the hardest part of this system. And you have cleared up a nagging financial stressor. Well done.

> ☑ **TAKE QUICK ACTION**
> The first step in channeling your magnificent money habit is opening one account. That's it. One account. One designation. One small step in setting up your Money Habit, one giant leap toward financial independence. Do this now. Not later. Not when you have time.

Set Up Your Accounts

Kari Saddler, who agreed to give the Money Habit system a shot, told me she was "two parts skeptical and one part willing to try because [she] felt like [she] was failing with money for so long." But after just two weeks of using the system, Kari still had money in her usual account for a grocery run, *plus* her WANTS account had more than enough for her fave sushi place and a movie. She said that normally, by that point in the month, she'd be scrambling to move money around to cover overspending. This time, she wasn't. "I'm completely amazed at how different this money habit feels," Kari told me.

I think you will be amazed be too. With that one account set up, the rest is easy. Easy money, so to speak.

Set a date to open your remaining bank accounts. And if your favorite date is today, all the better. Checking accounts are appropriate for INCOME, NEEDS, and WANTS; savings accounts are best for your DREAMS, FIX/FUTURE, and EMERGENCY accounts.

Right now, you're likely depositing your income into the same account you use to pay your bills. You're going to separate those activities, which means if you designate your current checking account as the INCOME account, you'll have to move any auto-payments for bills to the new NEEDS account. Or, if you'd rather designate your current checking account as the NEEDS account, you'll have to change the account into which your paycheck is deposited, so it goes into your new INCOME account. Either way, you can use the account(s) you already have to get started on the core six accounts.

At this point, just focus on getting the six-account structure in place. Later, you may choose to add more accounts or give them different names (which we'll talk about in chapter 5). Right now, it's as though you are laying the foundation for a house. You're not picking out paint colors yet; you're just pouring concrete.

When I was a kid, learning to tie my shoes felt like the ultimate hurdle in life. At least it felt that way to me. Over, under, pull it tight; make a bow and pull it right. That rhyme made it worse. I would make a knot. But then I just committed one day. I just did it over and over for a half hour, and voilà! I can tie my shoes for the rest of my life. Do it once, and you never need to do it again. That's what the Money Habit system is like.

The key is to realize that this is a one-time setup that pays off forever. The challenge is not the effort; it is the mental hurdle. For the half hour at the bank, or the thirteen minutes online, you will have a lifetime of financial independence.

But there is always an excuse that it can wait until tomorrow. So schedule it like your life depends on it, because it ... well, you know.

> ☑ **TAKE QUICK ACTION**
> Right now, schedule an appointment with your bank. Pick a date and time like it is a meeting with your doctor. Take the time off from work. Just schedule it.

If you were one of those kids where the shoe-tying rhyme actually worked, here's the one for your wealth: "Join the rank and go to the bank. Set up the accounts and boost your amounts."

If you're wondering about bank fees, remember that banks are vendors and you are their client. They are designed to serve you. If your current bank charges fees, ask them to waive them. Bank fees and minimum balances are annoying roadblocks, but they're completely avoidable with the right approach. First, choose a bank that works for you, not against you. Go to mymoneyhabit.com to get a list of banks I personally use and highly recommend and to see how they work with The Money Habit.

And if you're wondering what to say to the bank, here's an easy script: "I want to open six bank accounts so that I can manage my personal finances more effectively. I will be transferring money between these accounts regularly, so I need accounts that have no fees and no minimum balances."

Sixty-Six Days to Get the Hang of It

We've been talking a lot about habits, how we're naturally wired. We're working with what you already do, not asking you to become someone else. That said, we can learn how long it takes to create a habit and use that as a guidepost for how long it may take you to get the hang of the Money Habit system.

Most people think it takes twenty-one days to create a habit, but that's actually how long it takes to establish the routine. No wonder we have a hard time sticking to habits; we think we should have it down in three weeks, but it's not that simple.

Phillippa Lally's habit formation study discovered that it takes an average of sixty-six days to form a habit. Maybe it will take you a little more time, because some habits are harder to establish. Yours is simple. You're looking at your bank accounts every day, or whenever you need to spend money. Not that difficult!

So, check your calendar and make note of the date sixty-six days from now. That's when I want you to email me again and tell me how it's going. Make sure you write "66 Days of My Money Habit" in the subject line so I can find it. And as a reward, I will give you a bonus chapter that unlocks *only* when you've completed the full sixty-six days. No cheating. (That's a hint about the bonus chapter. You'll understand what I mean in nine weeks and three days.)

GET 'ER DONE SUMMARY
SET IT UP ONCE. LIVE IT FOREVER.

1. **Complete the One Account Challenge. Now!** Pick the biggest financial stressor or desire. Name it. Open a new account for it and label it (N-Rent, W-Dinner Out, D-New Outfit, you get the idea). One account. One purpose. One giant leap forward.

2. **Build your six-account system.** You're already opening one account, so keep the momentum going. Set up the six core accounts: INCOME, NEEDS, WANTS, DREAMS, FIX/FUTURE, and EMERGENCY. This is your money command center. Even if you don't use them all right away, the hard part of getting them set up is done.

3. **Schedule your wealthy weekday.** Pick one day a week to log in, allocate, and take a four-minute (or less) money pulse. Put it on your calendar like a meeting with your future self, because it is.

3

Align Your Money Target With Your Financial Season

DONNA LIM spread the white envelopes out on the kitchen table. Each one was rumpled from frequent use and had a label written in blue pen: Health Insurance, Mortgage, Food, Other Supplies, Prescriptions, Phone, Gas, School Lunch and Fees, Car Insurance, Cable TV, Clothes. Some envelopes were stuffed with tens and twenties, some just had a few dollar bills, and some were empty.

She looked at the faces of her husband and their two children and said, "Okay, everyone gets a vote. Which expense are we going to cut this week?"

Donna never expected to be in dire financial straits. In 2008, when the environmental health and safety industry started hiring independent contractors to save money, her husband lost his job. She had a three-year-old bookkeeping business that had made their family of four a little extra money, what she had called "the difference between hamburger and steak." But her husband had been the main breadwinner and her $28,000 in income a year could not come close to supporting their living in Silicon Valley. Especially because they had an extra set of required expenses related to her husband's poor health. It wasn't long before they had blown through their savings and didn't have enough money to cover their bills.

When Donna and her family voted on which expense to "vote off the island," as she puts it, they knew the first three bills to be paid were health insurance, food, and the mortgage, in that order. "This was before the Affordable Care Act," Donna explained, "when an insurance company could deny you coverage for a pre-existing condition, so we had to cover the health insurance first."

Donna worked hard to get more clients, but it wasn't enough. Her husband worked every day to find a new job, but no one was hiring. Eventually, he decided to change professions and learned graphic design so he could take on any job that would give them some income. They sold what they could: clothes, jewelry, furniture, sports equipment, electronics, whatever anyone would buy. To make matters worse, Donna's husband's health continued to decline. "Our church would call and ask, 'What do you need?' And I would say, 'Can someone just go pay for his insulin?'"

Despite all their efforts, and despite support from their community, eventually that envelope that was always third in line, the one labeled Mortgage, was completely empty. They got behind on their payments for their duplex, and then more behind, until finally the bank was involved. At the time, many people were in financial hell. A staggering 133,223 bankruptcy filings were recorded in California that year and of the twenty duplexes in Donna's area, eighteen were owned by the bank. *Eighteen.* She and her family were not alone. But that didn't make their situation any easier.

Desperation brought about an unthinkable idea. "I talked with my husband about splitting up the family. He'd take our oldest and sleep in the car. I'd take the younger one and sleep in the van."

Donna and her husband managed to come up with enough money to keep paying their mortgage, but they didn't have enough to cover the months they hadn't paid. Their foreclosure day turned out to be the same day as their wedding anniversary. As they waited for the sheriffs to come escort them out, Donna looked at her nearly empty home; they had sold almost everything.

Suddenly, like in a movie when the reprieve arrives just in time, her attorney called to say the bank agreed to let them stay in the home and pay off the unpaid debt over time.

That was a turning point, the start of a new season, one focused on recovery. Over time, all the envelopes filled with cash, and eventually, when Donna started using Profit First, the envelopes became bank accounts. Donna would move out of recovery mode and into other new seasons, where she focused on other goals beyond mere survival.

One of the reasons many financial habits don't stick is because life is not static. We experience good years and super lean years, tragedy and good fortune. Our needs and goals change as we make big life decisions, like having children and later, launching them into the world. Like the winter melting into spring, we move from one financial season into another. Nothing is permanent. So we need a money management system that moves with us from season to season.

The Four Financial Seasons

I often write to "The Four Seasons" by Antonio Vivaldi, four violin concertos, one for each season: winter, spring, summer, and fall. Even if you think you don't know the piece, you've heard it in movies and in commercials. I'm far more of an '80s hair bands fan, personally. You know, the good stuff, like when you're rockin' to Dokken or crankin' Autograph. But Vivaldi's music? It's "turn it up" great.

It turns out "The Four Seasons" was the first composition based on stories (sonnets). Pretty cool. Like Vivaldi's piece, there are four financial seasons: Recover, Fund, Activate, and Balance, and a story behind each. And in every good story, there's a quest, a big goal the characters are trying to achieve.

So, in homage to Vivaldi, let's break down the story behind each of the four financial seasons.

Recover

This season is a rebuilding story. Maybe you had a big financial loss, such as a layoff, or a natural disaster. Maybe you're starting over after a divorce or bankruptcy. Or maybe your debt simply got out of hand. You'll know you're in the Recover season if you have ongoing debt that is over and above your mortgage for your primary residence. Or if your overall debt, including your mortgage, is growing. Let debt go, so your future can glow. It's recovery time.

Here are indicators you may be in the Recover season:

- Debt overload: You are carrying credit card balances, personal loans, medical bills, payday loans, or any other balance due.

- Poor credit score: If your credit score is lower than 580, you are considered a high-risk borrower, and we need to fix that.

- Tax debt: You owe back taxes to the government, risking penalties and wage garnishments.

- Recurring overdraft and banking fees: You are in a cycle of negative account balances and fees.

- Repossession and foreclosure: You are at risk of losing or have lost a car or home due to past financial mismanagement.

- Student loan crisis: You carry a heavy debt burden from past education choices.

- Co-signed loan gone wrong: You are stuck paying for someone else's defaulted loan. (This almost happened to me. A former girlfriend who couldn't get a loan "begged" me to co-sign. I declined and lost the girl. Thank G! I guess it wasn't much of a relationship. I was just a source of money—when I was in college, with *no* money!)

- Any other financial hangovers: You bought a house, car, or business that became a money pit. Or you have debt to anyone that you are struggling to pay.

Fund

This season is a dream-fulfillment story. You're saving for something you want in the future, either something just a few years out, like a new car, or something further out, like retirement or a vacation home. An indicator that you're in the Fund season is that you are adjusting your NEEDS and WANTS accounts down to *temporarily* pour more money into saving for something big. You are delaying short-term gratification in the present for future long-term happiness. If your Rainy Day fund is bone dry, that's another indicator that you're in the Fund season. A little each day brings dreams your way. It's funding time.

Here are indicators you may be in the Fund season:

- Building a robust emergency fund: You want to ensure life's surprises don't derail finances.

- Preparing for retirement: You invest in 401(k), IRA, or other future income sources.

- Saving for something big: You are saving up in anticipation of a large spend on something big in the not-so-distant future; for example, a down payment on a home or a property investment. Fund now and Activate soon.

- Building a college fund for kids: You are anticipating tuition costs so your children don't have to rely on loans.

- Preparing for an entrepreneurial investment: You are saving up to start a business or side hustle. Yippee!!! Entrepreneurship is my fave.

- Planning for long-term health care: You are preparing for medical costs, disability, or aging care.

- Planning for big life goals and dreams: You are planning ahead to fund travel, a sabbatical, passion project, or simply a fulfilling life.

Activate

This season is a "live it up" story. You're reducing your cash position to extract more experiences out of life now. Maybe you're going on that Disney family vacation or using your money to buy more time to relax and take care of yourself. Maybe you are paying for college. Or maybe you need the cash to support an aging family member. An indicator that you are in the Activate season is that you see every minute as more valuable than every dollar. Live each day your chosen way. It's activation time!

Here are indicators you may be in the Activate season:

- Time more than money: Experiences, moments, and being present are your priority over saving or making more money. You're directing money toward travel, hobbies, dining out, or personal passions rather than maximizing savings.

- Lifestyle upgrade: You're investing in a better home, a car, or quality-of-life improvements that enhance your daily experience.

- Personal growth: You're investing in education, courses, fitness, or self-improvement that enriches your current life.

- Generous giving: You're contributing to charities, supporting family members, or engaging in philanthropy without financial stress.

- The start of that entrepreneurial thing: You're launching or expanding a business, taking strategic financial risks to create something meaningful. *Noice!* It's go time!

- Comfortable cash flow: You're covering all your needs with ease and using extra funds for wants, rather than aggressively saving or paying down debt.

- Luxury and indulgences: You're allowing yourself to enjoy finer things, whether it's designer clothes, gourmet meals, or exclusive experiences.

- Home and space enhancements: You're remodeling, redecorating, or making non-essential improvements to your living environment.

- Spontaneous or big-picture spending: You're making a major purchase without stressing about the financial impact, knowing you're stable. This is an instance when the Activate season may be for a short period, even just a day. For example, you may be allocating in the Fund season, but you do one big spend (Activate) and then go back to Fund.

Balance

This season is a "best of both worlds" story. You're leaning into the now (Activate) while also saving for something cool in the future (Fund). You want the eight-dollar coffee, *and* you want to save for a down payment on a house. An indicator that you are in a Balance season is you have one eye on today and one eye on tomorrow. You don't feel 100 percent comfortable extracting a lot of cash for fun stuff, but you do feel comfortable enough to stop squirreling it all away. Save and spend, a blend that won't end. It's balance time.

Here are indicators you may be in the Balance season:

- Every dollar is doing something that feels right: You enjoy today's pleasures while ensuring tomorrow is secure. Every dollar has a purpose, whether it's for now or later.

- You are here now and ready for later: You indulge in experiences and purchases without that nagging fear of "Will this hurt me later?"

- You have a protective financial cushion: Your savings and emergency funds remain strong, allowing you to embrace the now without jeopardizing the future.

- You are investing in both experiences and security: You take the vacation but also contribute to retirement. You enjoy the good meal but still build your nest egg.

- You make calculated trade-offs, not sacrifices: You may choose a luxury purchase, but not at the expense of long-term peace of mind. You blend joy with responsibility.

- You are not second-guessing financial decisions: You're at ease knowing you're getting the most out of your money while ensuring security down the road.

- You have a financial rhythm: You aren't called to save aggressively (Fund) or spend freely (Activate). You've found a rhythm that feels right.

Balance does not mean you are putting the same amount or percentage into WANTS and DREAMS accounts. It simply means emotionally, you're in the middle. You are striking a balance between living optimally within your means in the day-to-day and saving deeply for one day in the future.

The Next Season
These financial seasons don't follow a fixed order, like spring leads to summer and so on. With financial seasons, you can go right from fall to spring and then back to fall, for example. Now if only that happened with weather in my neck of the woods! Goodbye endless shoveling in the winter!

Your next season is just that: the next season.

As I am clicking away at my keyboard, Krista and I are currently shifting from an Activate season into the Balance season. We are saving 36 percent of our income for retirement and future cash reserves, and 26 percent goes into "now" moments, like a long-overdue home renovation project and our annual two-week vacation to Long Beach Island (meet you at the Dairy King!).

Eventually, as we get older and decide to lean even more into the now, we will return to the Activate season. But right now, we are still focused on expanding our financial security. We don't want to worry if Social Security will still exist when we're sixty-five. And we don't want to be dependent on our kids when neither of us is drawing an income.

One final thought on seasons. In nature, they just happen. Winter's coming whether you want it or not and so is summer. But you do have some control. You can choose where to live. Love winter? Head way up north and enjoy it year-round. Prefer summer? The tropics might be your vibe. But no matter where you go, there's still some unpredictability. Storms roll in, plans get disrupted.

Financial seasons work the same way. You can choose to live in a stage such as Balance and plan your next move, maybe toward Activate. But life happens. Rugs get pulled out from under you. You might find yourself in Recover unexpectedly. This system, guided by The Money Target, gives you the power to live in the season you want and handle any season that comes your way. When an unforeseen season shows up, you're ready to adapt.

The Money Target

John Harrison was an eighteenth-century carpenter and clockmaker who saw a serious problem that needed to be fixed. Sailors faced a dire challenge: accurately determining longitude. They couldn't figure out how far west or east they were while at sea. To put this in more modern terms, imagine you board a flight from Seattle to Orlando. The captain would know if they had taken you far enough south but have no idea if they had gone as far east as they needed to. So you might land in Albuquerque or Dallas, or maybe they would overshoot Florida by a few hundred miles, and you would land in the Atlantic. In other words, not a good situation.

Because captains and crews didn't have a way to measure longitude, ships were lost at sea, causing countless sailors to perish and countless fortunes to be lost. In desperation, the British government established a prize for anyone who could solve the problem. Many believed the solution lay in celestial observations, but Harrison thought differently. He defined his own parameters: a clock so precise it could keep time despite a ship's rolling motion and temperature changes. The chronometer kept the exact time in Greenwich, England. This is why you may have heard of GMT, Greenwich Mean Time.

Using the chronometer, sailors could compare the time of day (by looking at the sun's position) or night (by observation of the stars) and compare it to the time in GMT. The time difference would reveal the distance east or west from Greenwich. With a few more calculations, they knew how far east or west they should travel. Like if you said you live in San Francisco and I said I am three hours ahead of you, you would know that I am somewhere on the east coast.

The chronometer became the thing to measure progress on a voyage, always telling you how far you had traveled, and you could also determine how far you still needed to go.

Here's the part that might just blow your mind, like it did mine. The chronometer's concept is still in use today, and you're using it every time you use GPS. Instead of comparing time with Greenwich, GPS compares time with multiple satellites down to nanoseconds. This precision pinpoints exactly where you are. Beacons are everywhere, guiding us and pinpointing us in our journey, just like Harrison's invention once did for sailors at sea. Just like The Money Target does for fattening your wallet.

The Money Target is a simple chart used to identify exactly what percentage of your income to allocate to each of your five bank accounts. The chart is based on what financially fit people do at all different levels of income and in different seasons. With it, you can determine exactly what your accounts and subsequent spending behaviors should be.

Admittedly, this is not a perfect science; a multitude of factors can affect the numbers, such as the costs of where you live and the size of your family. But don't get deterred by the details. The Money Target is like horseshoes or, apparently, parallel parking: Close enough is close enough.

Note: You won't find the INCOME account in the tables below because it disburses to all the other accounts.

Money Target Allocations

The following charts show the ideal percentage allocations based on your useable household income and financial season. In chapter 4, you will plug the percentages based on your tier into a tool called The Money Map to see how your current spending can shift toward optimal use.

Note re FIX/FUTURE: Once all debt (excluding your mortgage and other appreciating asset debts) is eliminated, the allocation stays the same, but the account is renamed from FIX to FUTURE.

TIER 1 INCOME: UP TO $50,000

	Recover	Fund	Activate	Balance
Needs	80%	80%	80%	80%
Wants	1%	2%	12%	8%
Dreams	1%	5%	4%	5%
Fix/Future	15%	8%	2%	4%
Emergency	3%	5%	2%	3%

TIER 2 INCOME: $50,001 TO $150,000

	Recover	Fund	Activate	Balance
Needs	65%	65%	65%	65%
Wants	10%	12%	25%	19%
Dreams	3%	11%	5%	8%
Fix/Future	20%	7%	3%	4%
Emergency	2%	5%	2%	4%

TIER 3 INCOME: $150,001 TO $300,000

	Recover	Fund	Activate	Balance
Needs	50%	50%	50%	50%
Wants	18%	14%	36%	25%
Dreams	5%	18%	9%	14%
Fix/Future	22%	10%	3%	6%
Emergency	5%	8%	2%	5%

TIER 4 INCOME: $300,001 TO $500,000

	Recover	Fund	Activate	Balance
Needs	35%	35%	35%	35%
Wants	22%	25%	40%	31%
Dreams	8%	20%	15%	18%
Fix/Future	25%	12%	5%	10%
Emergency	10%	8%	5%	6%

TIER 5 INCOME: $500,001 TO $1,000,000

	Recover	Fund	Activate	Balance
Needs	25%	25%	25%	25%
Wants	27%	21%	49%	31%
Dreams	11%	27%	16%	24%
Fix/Future	21%	16%	5%	11%
Emergency	16%	11%	5%	9%

TIER 6 INCOME: $1,000,001 AND UP

	Recover	Fund	Activate	Balance
Needs	20%	20%	20%	20%
Wants	30%	25%	65%	40%
Dreams	15%	30%	5%	22%
Fix/Future	20%	15%	5%	10%
Emergency	15%	10%	5%	8%

Here's how to use The Money Target.

Step 1: Identify Your Tier

Find your tier based on your annual, usable household income. This is the total net income from all individuals contributing to your household.

Step 2: Identify Your Financial Season

Identify your household's financial season using the definitions provided earlier in this chapter.

Step 3: Allocate Percentages to Your Foundational Accounts

Based on your current tier and financial season, assign percentages of your income to your foundational accounts. Remember, we want the system to show your financial circumstances within a few seconds of logging into your bank account. So, if you are in Tier 2 and in the Activate season, you would allocate 65 percent of your income to the NEEDS account. To give yourself instant clarity every time you login to your online banking, include both the account's purpose and its income allocation percentage in the account nickname. So instead of just naming it "NEEDS," call it "NEEDS (65%)."

Step 4: Review Your Season Regularly

Choose how often you want to review The Money Target to determine when you want to move into a new season. Weekly reviews, like Finance Friday or Money Monday, ensure consistency, while quarterly check-ins allow you to reassess your season and adjust percentages as needed.

By adhering to the Money Target tool, you'll become clear and empowered. You will know where you stand and how much further you need to travel. Each adjustment will bring you closer to the financial parameters that work seamlessly with your life. Let The Money Target be your chronometer.

> ☑ **TAKE QUICK ACTION**
> Choose your financial season. If you don't know what season you are in, start with Recover. The system is designed so that the seasons will reveal themselves as you move along. So just get 'er started with Recover. Wipe out your debt and build your foundation by transitioning into Fund.

When Your Income Is Unpredictable

Your income might bounce around like my old cat's mood, purring one minute, scratching the bejesus out of me the next. Maybe you're on commission, work hourly shifts, or run a seasonal business. Whatever the cause of the income swings, The Money Target still works. In fact, it might work even better for you, because it gives every dollar a job the moment it lands.

Here's how to make it simple and sustainable:

Step 1: Set Your Floor

Look back at the past twelve months and find your lowest-earning month. That's your floor, your worst-case scenario. Multiply that month's income by twelve, and that becomes your tier for The Money Target. Why? Because if you can build your system around your worst month, then anything above that becomes pure financial momentum.

Step 2: Prioritize Survival First

If your income is unpredictable, start with one of these financial seasons: Recover, Fund, or Balance. Avoid Activate for now, unless you already have large amounts of savings. Activate is designed for people with consistent, predictable income or substantial savings and encourages spending money based on consistent access. That's too risky when you're unsure of what's coming next. But no worries, you will be able to activate the spend soon enough.

By operating from your floor, you ensure security first. When you have a strong month, the system doesn't encourage a spending spree (which is the big danger, equivalent to when my cat goes for my face). Instead, a strong month helps you stockpile for when the pendulum swings back, so you're not left scrambling during leaner months.

Step 3: Give It Twelve Months

Once you've used this approach for a full year, you'll have a much clearer view of your real financial landscape. And assuming you have strong months, not just floor months, you will automatically have set aside cash. This is when you can allocate the excess dough. Maybe it goes into accumulating savings, paying necessary bills, or spending on the things you want to make happen next year.

You're not officially in the Activate season, but you're giving yourself permission to *activate* some of those funds.

Step 4: Recalculate Yearly

Every twelve months:

1. Recalculate your floor based on the new twelve-month cycle.
2. Adjust your tier if needed.

3 Move to (or stay in) the season that fits your current reality. This includes the option of moving into the Activate season.
4 Use the excess money for intentional spending based on last year's overages, not on this month's optimism.

This approach gives you flexibility *without sacrificing stability*. You're still living within your means, still protecting your financial future, and still building momentum one varying deposit at a time.

> ☑ **TAKE QUICK ACTION**
> When you consider your Money Target allocations, base your starting point upon your floor income and your season, and then live by them consistently. As a result, every dollar earned over your floor becomes your win.

When The Money Target Feels Out of Reach

What do you do if your Money Target doesn't seem doable right now? The good news: You're not alone. Many folks feel adjusting to the target percentages is too much too fast. The great news: The fix is easy and is designed to move at a manageable pace.

Step 1: Review Your Spending
Look at your historical spending to see what percentage of your income you currently allocate to NEEDS, WANTS, DREAMS, FIX/FUTURE, and EMERGENCY accounts. (I'll show you exactly how to do this in the next chapter.)

Step 2: Calculate Your Typical Percentages
Compare the percentages from your historical spending to the Money Target standards.

Step 3: Slowly Close the Gap

Don't force yourself to hit the target percentages on day one. Over the course of two years, aim to shift your income and your allocations. Review and shift your percentages every ninety days (every quarter) so that you are inching toward the Money Target allocations that match your income and your season. This phased approach reduces the strain that can come from doing it true and blue from the get-go. For many, starting slow and letting it grow is the best approach. Life happens. Economies shift; jobs come and go. While two years is the guideline, adjust as needed. Just don't ever, ever, ever abandon the system. Cool? Cool.

Step 4: Notice Any Financial Strain

As you work toward closing the gap, pay attention to any financial strain. If you hit a ceiling where adjusting further feels too tight, pause for a quarter before reassessing. Progress isn't about speed; it's about sustainability. Sometimes the raise doesn't happen or inflation does, and not-so-pleasant life surprises (like job loss) can stretch the timeline. The key is to keep moving forward at a pace that keeps you financially stable and stress-free.

Of course, there are the hardcore folks, the people who want to set up the entire system immediately. For the folks like that who would rather go all in and get the hard stuff over fast, starting out and sticking with the Money Target percentages from day one is the way to go. With this approach, you will get the benefits fast.

Adapting to Your Season

Changing seasons, whether due to a new job, unexpected windfall, financial setback, or a new chapter in your life, will require adjustments to your Money Target allocations. Here's what to concentrate on in each season:

- Recover—Prioritize NEEDS and FIX. Address critical expenses like rent, utilities, and groceries while actively paying down debt.

- Fund—Focus on setting aside cash to DREAMS and FUTURE. Build long-term savings for significant goals like retirement or a down payment.

- Activate—Shift your attention to building WANTS and drawing funds from DREAMS. Allocate cash for meaningful experiences, such as vacations or personal goals, while staying within your means.

- Balance—Blend WANTS, DREAMS, and FUTURE. This is about finding harmony, where you're enjoying life today while preparing for tomorrow.

Here are a few things you can do to spot when a change in season may be in order:

- Check your numbers. Your bank accounts tell the story. If your NEEDS account is always tight while your DREAMS account grows, you may be overfunding the future (Fund season) and are preparing to shift into Activate. If debt lingers stubbornly, you're still in Recover.

- Monitor stress levels. Financial stress is a powerful indicator. If you're panicked about bills, you're likely in Recover. If cash is piling up but you feel restricted, you may be overdue for Activate.

- Reflect on your goals. What's your current focus? Paying off debt signals Recover. Saving for a dream aligns with Fund. Prioritizing enjoyment points to Activate. A thirst for living in the now while also securing your future indicates Balance. Your goals clarify your season.

- Be honest about shifts. Seasons can change suddenly. Did a windfall boost your savings? Did an emergency drain your funds? Stay alert to life's changes and adjust your strategy accordingly.

Financial seasons don't control you. Winter may be brutal, but it's temporary. Fall takes effort, but the rewards are worth it. Spring brings growth, and summer offers joy. The key is recognizing your season and adapting your Money Target to match.

The Beauty and Work of Recover Season

Where I live in New Jersey, winter can be the most beautiful of seasons. After a snowstorm, the world transforms into a white, fresh, heavenly landscape. Powder glistens like diamonds under the sun, and a quiet stillness blankets everything, inviting a momentary pause in life. I cozy up in a chair with tea or on rare occasions a bourbon, and on super rare occasions, a bourbon tea (don't judge, it's a thing).

But winter is also demanding. The shoveling! Oh, that @#$%! shoveling! Hours of back-breaking work to clear paths, dig out the car, only to witness the @#$%! snowplow guy burying my driveway entrance with packed ice boulders. Thanks, pal. I hope you're enjoying that "hot chocolate" of yours, which we all know is bourbon tea.

Freezing fingers, numb toes, and the sharp sting of cold makes every effort a challenge. Winter is a mix of bleak and beauty, a promise of renewal that must be earned.

Sam Horton-Martin was in the depths of his financial winter. Over the years, I've come to know Sam as the essence of a good guy. He does anything for a friend. He had a wonderful marriage that he cherished deeply. His husband, Wayne, was the financial anchor in their relationship, and when he passed away, Sam was devastated. Emotionally and financially. His husband left him hundreds of thousands of dollars in his will, a gift meant to protect Sam and secure his future.

Within three years, Sam lost it all.

By the time Sam and I spoke, he was in his bleakest hour. His bank account held literal pennies. He was living off food stamps and handouts from friends. His rent was months overdue, and his landlords, whom Sam had become close with during the pandemic, faced the agonizing decision of evicting a good man or sacrificing their own source of income.

But worse than the financial wreckage was Sam's shame. He felt he had disrespected his husband's hopes for him, destroyed the gift he had been entrusted with, and proved to himself that he was incapable of handling money. His winter wasn't powdery snow and diamonds; it was slush, ice, and salt. Not the plow guy's road salt, but the salt that gets rubbed into wounds.

Then The Money Habit changed everything. Because the key to Sam's financial transformation, and quite possibly yours, is not cash; it's clarity.

Sam's struggles weren't just about having too little money, though he had practically none. The real challenge was the paralysis he felt from not knowing what to do with what he did have. Without clarity, everything feels insurmountable. Sam's reaction to the uncertainty was to shut down and freeze up, even awkwardly "laughing away" his money concerns by labeling himself as a "money moron" and "sucking at math."

The first mission when you're feeling stuck is to recognize the root of the problem: a lack of clarity.

Research indicates that the fear of uncertainty can be more distressing than facing a known adverse outcome. A study published in *Social Science & Medicine* found that people often experience greater anxiety waiting for medical test results than they do when receiving a serious diagnosis. The not-knowing creates a worry spiral, where you imagine the worst-case scenarios, while knowing, even if the facts are dire, brings clarity and the ability to act.

Money works the same way. It's not the problem itself that's most frightening; it's the uncertainty of not knowing where you stand or where you need to go. Once you have clarity, you can start the march forward and experience, maybe the first time in forever, confidence that you have control over money.

Clarity Through Focus

We got busy diagnosing Sam's financial situation. He had debt piled up and couldn't pay all his bills: classic signs of the cold, harsh Recover season. First, we analyzed his income. With his part-time coding job, Sam fell into Tier 1 on The Money Target. We then ran the percentages and found there was just enough (barely enough) to cover his essentials while still chipping away at his debt. Funding indulgences or emergency savings? Nearly impossible at this stage. The mind thirsts reward. Even in the Recover season, the WANTS account still gets a few dollars every week if that is all we can spare. It's minimal, but it keeps motivation alive.

With this target plan in place, it became clear: Cutting costs alone wouldn't make Sam financially fit. He needed to increase his income by moving from part time to more "time" and less "part." At least to the extent his health allowed.

Next, we tackled clarity through accounts, which is something you'll need too. We always begin with the six starter accounts: INCOME, NEEDS, WANTS, DREAMS, FIX/FUTURE, and EMERGENCY. But real peace of mind comes when you zoom in and tailor those accounts to fit your current financial season. In chapter 5, I'll share more about how Sam used the Money Habit system to move from crisis to recovery.

Saving Too Much

About thirty-five miles south of where Sam lives is Tiffany Aliche, the brilliant author of *Get Good with Money*. When I committed to writing this book, Tiffany was one of my first calls. Why? Because I knew she'd bring the goods. Tiffany has this incredible way of making you rethink everything you thought you knew about money. I wanted her take, her sharp insights on how we deal with our finances and how we (mis)behave when it comes to them. And, man, she delivered. Her ideas poured out like water from a firehose, each one sparking new thoughts for this book.

But here's what really hit me: It wasn't just her ideas. It was her *story*. Like a lot of people, I'd always assumed the toughest part of financial growth was building funds to climb out of debt, save for dreams, or stack up investments. But Tiffany shattered that notion with something I'd overlooked entirely: the miser's problem. When saving becomes the sole obsession, living gets pushed to the sidelines. And in that moment, I saw it crystal clear! Financial freedom isn't just about accumulating; it's about living. In retrospect, it was a no, duh! She was reminding me of a premise that you and I both already know: the caveman principle. We gather, store, and use. Well, we are *supposed* to use.

"So, one day my parents sat me down," Tiffany shared, "and they were like, 'Is everything okay?' I was confused. 'Yeah, why?' They said, 'You look... you look like hell.'"

Tiffany said Nigerians are direct, and Nigerian parents are really, really direct. Their bluntness stung. Tiffany had been saving relentlessly, skipping self-care and everyday spending to build her financial cushion. Tiffany briefly looked down at the "well-worn" outfit she had on, and her emotions swelled.

"I remember snapping back, 'I'm saving! I'm being responsible like you taught me!' And then my frugal parents, parents who taught me to save every penny, said something that shocked me: 'It's okay to spend some money, dear.'"

Her father, a man so financially disciplined he could make a spreadsheet blush, handed Tiffany his credit card and told her to go spend $400 at Macy's or Sears. "I knew something was wrong," she said, "when the cheapest man I know told me to treat myself to new clothes."

Ah yes, the miser. So infamous, that the last name of one of Charles Dickens's most famous characters, Ebenezer Scrooge, is now synonymous with being a miser. The miser syndrome is the obsessive tendency toward not so much saving as much as "not losing." There is a constant worry that spending of any type will lead to financial ruin. The consequences are avoiding spending on expenses that would actually improve quality of life. The emotional toll of guilt is too much to bear when the miser does spend.

John Elwes, a British member of parliament, in the eighteenth century, epitomized miser syndrome so completely that despite inheriting a vast fortune, he refused to spend money even on basic necessities. He lived in crumbling properties, wore clothes until they disintegrated, and ate spoiled food. His relentless pursuit of "not losing" drove him to sit in the dark to avoid the cost of candles. He even declined to pay for the most rudimentary education for his two sons, George and John, reasoning that "putting things into people's heads is the sure way to take money out of their pockets."

All this worry, and it could have been avoided (barring legitimate mental health issues) with The Money Habit. The system doesn't just show you where your money should go; it assigns it a purpose before you use it, freeing you from the mental gymnastics of "Am I using this the right way?" Each dollar knows its job. It's not just sitting there making you feel like a miser for spending it; it's at your bank, ready to get to work for you in the way you always intended. And with that, worry wilts. Hope that helps, Ebenezer.

Regain Agency

In August of 2023, Vickie Lanthier unexpectedly lost a "healthy" six-figure consulting contract. And just like that, she landed in a new financial season. At the time, she had $60,000 in commercial debt, as well as her mortgage and other living expenses. Most people would panic in a situation like this, but not Vickie. A fourteen-year military veteran, she knows how to survive a crisis.

In her book *High Agency Human*, Vickie details how she not only survived being drop-kicked into a Recover season, but eliminated the typical financial overwhelm most people feel when they lose their primary source of income. She used a process she developed called Radical Reduction, where she instantly reduced her expenses down to just the fundamentals. The essence of her system? No delays. No overthinking. Just do it. And just do it once. Hard.

Within ten days, she had sold her house and moved into an apartment, sold some of her furniture and other items that did not fit into her apartment, and eliminated expenses she didn't need. Through this process, she cleared her debt, created a $20,000 emergency fund, and increased her investment savings by $100,000.

The combination of the mass liquidation and reduced ongoing expenses left her with extra cash to fund a life pivot over the next year, which she used to obtain her registered nurse license and get a new job. And thanks to some creative moves, she also took her dream trip to the Arctic and went to France for the eightieth anniversary of D-Day.

By moving quickly, Vickie was able to shift into a new season and a new life. When I asked her how she could let go of so much, she explained people get caught up in the sunk-cost fallacy, our cognitive bias to continue to spend money on something we've already invested in, like a big house, even when it no longer makes sense to do so.

Vickie said something that has stuck with me and speaks to the heart of the Money Habit system: "We need to live at the limits that set us free. This is how we gain agency over our own lives." When you choose your financial limits, on purpose, a magical thing happens. Chaos converts to structure, structure sharpens clarity, and clarity creates freedom.

Back on the Lim

When I met Donna Lim for the first time, she shook my hand and said, "I hated your book."

"Youch. That's not good. Tell me more," I replied. "Why did you hate it?"

"Because of all those bank accounts."

Donna is now the founder of Sooter Consulting, an accounting firm that helps people improve their cash flow. She was referring to my book *Profit First*, which she had heard about from some of her clients who were implementing the method. To her, the accounts seemed confusing, unnecessary, and like "a lot more work."

The second time she heard about it, she ignored it. By the third time, she said, "Okay, this system isn't going to go away, so let me really understand it." The fourth time a client mentioned it, she decided to try it herself.

"I did your one percent challenge," she said, "and I never looked back."

(Donna is referring to my challenge to *Profit First* readers to transfer 1 percent of their income into a PROFIT account. I adapted that challenge for you; it's the one account challenge from the previous chapter. If you haven't completed it, this is your cue. I don't care if you're in your undies! Go do it now!)

She shared her story with me, the envelope survivor story I shared with you at the start of this chapter. Today, she is a certified Profit First Professional who swears by "all those bank accounts." She's seen the system transform her clients' businesses and her own. "I don't know why starting the bank accounts was so hard for me at first," she said, "because I had used the envelope system to get us through that terrible time."

Donna stood at the edge of financial collapse, juggling bills and planning how to keep her family safe without a home. Yet, with the envelope system, step by step, she fought back. She modernized the physical envelopes into multiple bank accounts and tackled her finances with clarity.

I think my favorite part of her story involves that same set of envelopes, laid out on the dining table. It was when, for the first time in ages, a little extra money appeared.

Gathering her family around the table, Donna asked a simple question: "We have a bit more now. What do you want to bring back into our lives?"

She expected her kids to request cable TV, gadgets, or maybe a well-deserved dinner out for the family. But their answer was humbling in its simplicity: "Mom, can you just go to Costco and stock the kitchen like you used to?"

Ah, yes, the abundance of a full cupboard. There's more to it than food, it's the security of knowing there's enough, always. In that moment, Donna realized the true power of her season wasn't just climbing out of debt; it was creating a new foundation for her family to always have enough.

The Recover season isn't the end of Donna's story, nor is it yours. It's the beginning. Donna and Vickie are in the Fund season now. Tiffany is in Activate. I just entered the Balance season. Sam is navigating Recover. And you? What season is it for you? Whatever it is, embrace it, my friend. It's beautiful out there! Own the situation you're in, and lean into the reason for your season.

GET 'ER DONE SUMMARY
KNOW YOUR CURRENT SEASON.
BLAZE YOUR FINANCIAL FUTURE.

1 **Choose your financial season.** Are you rebuilding (Recover), stockpiling (Fund), enjoying the now (Activate), or doing a bit of both (Balance)? Don't overthink it, pick the one that fits today. Seasons change, and so will you.

2 **Use The Money Target.** Find your tier (based on take-home, usable household income), match it to your season, and apply the percentage allocations. These are your financial coordinates. Follow them.

3 **Name it to claim it.** Modify the labels of your bank accounts to include the allocation percentages (e.g., NEEDS [65%]). The percentages give you clarity on where your money goes. The accounts give every dollar a job. And every job gets done.

4

Plot Your Course on Your Money Map

EVERY YEAR, I visit my family doctor. I hope you do the same; it's the best way to track your health. Over the last five or ten years, something interesting happened during my annual blood tests. My doctor would tell me, "Your sugar levels are elevated. Stop eating sweets." I never really took it to heart. I'd laugh it off, thinking, *Well, I guess I have sweet blood.* Besides, I didn't think I ate many sweets. Sure, I binged on strawberry Twizzlers on every road trip "because it's not just the car, I need 'fuel' too," but it wasn't like I had them every day.

The prescription wasn't enough of a wake-up call. I needed something, apparently, on paper and in my face. I applied for a new life insurance policy and did not get elite health status. To give you context, I exercise five days a week. I do cardio and weights. I eat vegetables and fruits. I'm at a healthy weight for my height. I have very little stress. And I cold-plunge, which I mention not because there are any scientifically proven benefits, but like every plunger, I feel obliged to share it with the world. So there's that. By all measures, I thought I was in excellent shape. Except for my blood sugar.

When I got only standard qualifications for my life insurance, while a slightly, let's say "paunchy" friend (who I won't embarrass by revealing his real identity as Greg Eckler, my fraternity brother from Delta Sigma Pi, a 1994 graduate of Virginia Tech who now lives in Colorado, so I will call him Gerg... whoops! Sorry, Gerg) qualified for elite status with the same company, I was knocked out of my chair.

I called the insurance company and asked them why. They said, "Your blood sugar is too high."

Hearing it as a "you should do this" from my doctor wasn't enough to move me. But having that number right in front of me, not qualifying for something I thought I deserved, and seeing this was costing me money to boot, that was the wake-up call.

I launched a quick fourteen-day glucose study on myself. The main culprits? Two things: tons of bread and excessive dry fruit. My God, do I wolf down bread. And dried fruit? I can go through a bag of dried apples faster than the winner of a Nathan's Famous International Hot Dog Eating Contest. One shriveled apple has as much sugar as, you guessed it, one non-shriveled apple. One a day keeps the doctor away, but a bag of forty? In one day, I was eating an entire year of schoolteacher's bribes. Every day. And I thought it was healthy. But this experiment gave me the insights I needed to moderate. I simplified my diet and improved my sugar levels dramatically.

Now, let's talk about your finances. Just like with my blood sugar revelation, you need a health check. You now know about the financial seasons, and you've identified your tier with the Money Target system, so we have the information we need to take a close look at your current spending—and how you need to adjust it. We'll use a tool I call The Money Map. It works hand-in-hand with The Money Target, which gives us your financial destination.

The Money Map is your GPS. In no time, we'll determine the health of your current financial situation so we can plot a course for a healthy future. Bonus: This process doesn't require any needles, unlike my dang blood sugar tests.

The Money Map

If someone is planning to lose weight, the first step they need to take is to get their baseline. They need to know their heft and measurements. Great money management kicks off the same way: You need to know where you stand. The Money Map starts with your financial weigh-in.

Don't worry about nailing every detail or sweating the financial nuances, because that's not the goal here. We just need a ballpark idea of how much you make, how much you spend, and where that money goes. Even if you're clueless about the exact numbers, your best guesses are more than enough to get this system working fast.

You can do this on paper. Alternatively, all the tools you need for this are waiting for you at mymoneyhabit.com. Let's make this simple and get right to it. Here's how it works.

Step 1.0: Calculate Your Monthly Usable Income

The monthly usable income of your household (whether one income or more contributes to it) is the foundation of your personal finances. Since most bills and expenses hit monthly, we need to align your income the same way, to make it easy to compare what's coming in versus what's going out.

We will use the Monthly Usable Income Calculator to do the simple math. And, as an example throughout, we will follow the journey of a couple, Buck and Penny (you got me, it's Gerg), who are using the Money Habit system.

MONTHLY USABLE INCOME CALCULATOR

	Amount
Earner 1 annual take-home income	
Earner 2 annual take-home income	
Other annual take-home income	
Total annual usable income	
Divide by 12	**= monthly usable income**

Monthly Usable Income Calculator. Use this tool to total all sources of your annual household income. Then divide the total annual usable income by twelve to convert it to monthly income, making it easier to match the typical monthly rhythm of expenses.

Your take-home income is the actual amount that lands in your bank account *after* taxes, 401(k) contributions, insurance, and other deductions. In other words, it is the money that is usable. Just because your salary is $10,000 a month doesn't mean you get $10,000. It might be closer to $6,800. That's the number we work with.

- Earner 1 annual take-home income: Likely you or a significant other.

- Earner 2 annual take-home income: If you have a second household income, include it here. If not, leave it blank.

- Other annual take-home income: This includes any steady money coming in, such as child support payments, Social Security or pension payments, rental or investment income, other contributing household income, public benefits or aid, or that uncle who moved in "for just a few weeks" seven years ago. But at least he helps with the bills.

Once you've totaled your annual usable take-home income, divide it by twelve to get your monthly usable income (MUI, pronounced moo-ey, like a cow that demands extra attention. You know, *kinda moo-y*).

☑ **TAKE QUICK ACTION**
Calculate your MUI and round it to the nearest dollar. This isn't government bookkeeping. Close enough is good enough. Speed beats pinpoint accuracy here.

Let's see this in action with Buck and Penny. Penny earns $68,000 after taxes, Buck earns $54,000. They have no extra income and, lucky them, no freeloading uncle.

MONTHLY USABLE INCOME CALCULATOR

	Amount
Earner 1 annual take-home income	$68,000
Earner 2 annual take-home income	$54,000
Other annual take-home income	$0
Total annual usable income	**$122,000**
Divide by 12 = monthly usable income	**$10,167**

Monthly Usable Income Calculator (Buck and Penny). This example shows Buck and Penny's combined annual take-home income. The total is divided by twelve to calculate their monthly usable income. Important note: This reflects net income, the amount deposited after taxes and deductions, not their gross or top-line income.

Not sure what the actual take-home income is for you or another earner? Use one of these methods:

Ask your boss. Just say, "I'm taking better control of my finances. Can you provide my gross and net annual pay?" Most will happily help. Bonus ask of the boss: "Hey, while we are at it, how about that raise?" Proceed at your own risk.

Check your paystub. If you're paid weekly, multiply your net pay by fifty-two. If twice a month, multiply by twenty-four. If your paystub frequency is different or hard to calculate, the tools at mymoneyhabit.com will do it for you.

Look at your bank deposits. If your paycheck is direct deposited, this is your net pay. Identify the amount and frequency, then annualize it.

Use last year's W-2 (with a catch). This only shows gross wages. To find your net, ask the human resource folks or your accountant for a breakdown of your deductions.

Refer to last year's tax return. If you have variable income (self-employed income, commissions, etc.), use last year's tax return as a baseline, or divide the last twelve months of deposits by twelve.

If you or another earner stashes some income on the side *before* contributing to the household (Doomsday prepping? A hidden bug-out fund?) only count what actual contributions go to household operations.

Step 2.0: Calculate Your Total Monthly Spending

Understanding your total monthly expenses and savings shows where your net income is already committed. This is the most critical step in gaining financial clarity. It gives you a clear picture of your money flow.

Use this monthly money flow calculator to run your calculations. Start with the MUI you calculated in step 1, put it in the top row of the chart, and categorize it as INCOME.

Continuing Buck and Penny's example, we get the following:

MONTHLY MONEY FLOW CALCULATOR

Description	Amount	Category
Monthly usable income	$10,167	Income

Monthly Money Flow Calculator (Buck and Penny, income). The first entry in the Monthly Money Flow Calculator is your monthly usable income, copied directly from the Monthly Usable Income Calculator.

Step 2.1: Gather Your Expense Data

The next thing to do is to collect and categorize your expenses. Gather the following for the last three months (or just last month if that's all you have):

- Bank statements
- Credit card statements
- Receipts

In your Monthly Money Flow Calculator, write down your *regular* monthly expenses. Focus on monthly expenses first. Record the following:

- Description: What the expense is (e.g., rent, groceries, streaming subscriptions)
- Amount: The fixed monthly cost (e.g., rent, streaming subscription) or a rough average for variable costs (e.g., groceries).

Then tackle your *sporadic* expenses (e.g., dining out, vacations). Calculate your approximate annual spend on them. So, for three months of an expense, simply divide it by three to determine the monthly amount. If you spent $1,500 on dining out in three months (the way Buck and Penny did), the equation would look like this:

$1,500 ÷ 3 = $500

Record the description and the amount for your sporadic expenses in the flow calculator.

Here's what Buck and Penny's chart looks like now:

MONTHLY MONEY FLOW CALCULATOR

Description	Amount	Category
Monthly usable income	$10,167	Income
Rent	$4,000	
Groceries	$800	
Luxury car	$1,500	
Gas	$250	
Streaming subs	$150	
Dining out	$500	
New furniture	$525	
Credit card bill	$2,300	
Gifts	$75	
Gym membership	$450	
Vacation	$500	
Clothing	$250	

Monthly Money Flow Calculator (Buck and Penny, income and expenses). Each expense is itemized and assigned a monthly amount. Both fixed costs, such as rent, and estimated sporadic spending, such as gifts, are included. The wavy line at the bottom of the table signals that Buck and Penny may have additional expenses. When you fill out your own, make sure to include everything.

The reason we record all expenses and costs without tracking an ongoing balance is to prevent mental interference. When we see a running balance, we tend to second-guess or try to "improve" the system on the fly, which can distort the truth and undermine the process.

Step 2.2: Identify Categories
Now that everything is captured, it's time to categorize each expense and calculate the balance.

Assign each expense to a category: NEEDS, WANTS, DREAMS, FIX/FUTURE, or EMERGENCY.

- Be honest and discerning about the category assignment.
- Your mortgage is likely a NEED, unless it's for a second home, which might be a DREAM. (Even after you've saved enough to acquire a second home, unless you need it for survival, any bills related to that home are DREAM expenses.)
- Groceries are typically a NEED, dining out a WANT, and a personal chef is definitely a DREAM.
- As for clothing, you need it, sure, but anything Louis Vuitton is a WANT or DREAM, not a NEED.

Your critical review is essential. A friend or expert might provide even more objectivity. If I may, I suggest you connect with an expert, such as the Money Habit Mentors at the front of this book. You can find more support from our Profit First Professionals community at mymoneyhabit.com.

As a reminder:

- NEEDS: Essentials (rent, groceries, utilities)
- WANTS: Nice-to-haves (dining out, entertainment)
- DREAMS: Big goals (vacations, luxury items)
- FIX: Debt payments
- FUTURE: Savings/investments (or investing in your own growth)
- EMERGENCY: Unexpected expenses

Here's what it looks like for Buck and Penny:

MONTHLY MONEY FLOW CALCULATOR

Description	Amount	Category
Monthly usable income	$10,167	Income
Rent	$4,000	Need
Groceries	$800	Need
Luxury car	$1,500	Dream
Gas	$250	Need
Streaming subs	$150	Want
Dining out	$500	Want
New furniture	$525	Dream
Credit card bill	$2,300	Fix
Gifts	$75	Want
Gym membership	$450	Want
Vacation	$500	Dream
Clothing	$250	Need

Monthly Money Flow Calculator (Buck and Penny, categories complete). This chart shows Buck and Penny's monthly expenses sorted into the different Money Habit system categories.

If you're not currently allocating money to certain categories, that's a-okay. Right now we're simply getting a clear picture of how your money is being used. In Buck and Penny's case, there's no money going toward the FUTURE or EMERGENCY categories, and that's just fine.

Step 3.0: Total the Categories and Calculate Percentages

Now, let's break things down into The Money Map. The first goal is to total each category from the Monthly Money Flow Calculator and determine what percentage of your monthly income is going toward each one. Your category totals may exceed or fall short of your income. This is normal. So don't stress over this. The goal here is simply to understand the general trend of where your money is going, not to get everything perfect.

Continuing our case study of Buck and Penny, we see the totals add up as follows:

- NEEDS—$5,300 = rent ($4,000) + groceries ($800) + gas ($250) + clothing ($250)
- WANTS—$1,175 = streaming subscriptions ($150) + dining out ($500) + gifts ($75) + gym membership ($450)
- DREAMS—$2,525 = luxury car ($1,500) + new furniture ($525) + vacation ($500)
- FIX—$2,300 = credit card bill ($2,300)
- FUTURE—$0
- EMERGENCY—$0

Note that both the FIX and FUTURE categories are listed here. That's intentional. It's possible you've been trying to address two top priorities by paying off past debts while also trying to prepare for the future. For now, we need to assess both simultaneously to understand your full financial picture.

But when we implement the system, we'll shift focus. First priority: Clean up the past by tackling debt and overdue obligations (while still preparing for emergencies). Then, once we lift that weight, we will reroute more money toward the future by building savings, investing, and creating true financial momentum.

Calculate Percentages

To determine the percentage of your income allocated to each category, use this simple formula:

Category monthly total ÷ Income monthly total × 100 = percentage of income

Take Buck and Penny's NEEDS, for example:
$5,300 ÷ $10,167 × 100 = 52.1% → rounds down to 52%

Repeat this for all categories to get a clear picture of where your money is going. Once you have your numbers, plug them into The Money Map below.

THE MONEY MAP

	Monthly Total	Actual %	Target %	Adjust
Income	$10,167	N/A		
Needs	$5,300	52%		
Wants	$1,175	12%		
Dreams	$2,525	25%		
Fixes	$2,300	23%		
Future	$0	0%		
Emergency	$0	0%		
Totals	$11,300	112%		

The Money Map (Buck and Penny, first two columns complete). Transfer your Money Habit category totals from the Monthly Money Flow Calculator into the monthly total column here. Then insert each total's corresponding percentage of monthly income in the Actual % column. Add up all the category totals and percentages. Don't worry if, as with Buck and Penny's example, the percentages add up to more or less than 100 percent. That just indicates an opportunity for improvement.

Looking at the Money Map example, we see that Buck and Penny's total expenses exceed their income, meaning they're running a deficit. Since their spending is 112 percent of their income, they're outspending their earnings and will need adjustments.

However, your numbers might look different.

If your expenses are lower than income, then extra money is unaccounted for. That surplus could be allocated to FUTURE or EMERGENCY categories, depending on your priorities.

> ☑ **TAKE QUICK ACTION**
> When you look at your own numbers, if you find your running balance is negative (indicating you're running at a deficit and relying on debt to cover it), don't criticize yourself. That doesn't help. The goal is to gather the facts, just the facts, ma'am.

Step 3.1: Apply Money Target Percentages Based on Your Season

Now, refer to The Money Target in chapter 3. Find your current tier by identifying your annual household usable income. And recall your current financial season. Here's a quick refresher:

Recover: You have debt outside of asset-related loans like a mortgage or reasonable car payment and carry balances month to month. Your priority is regaining stability and reducing debt. (If you are unsure, start with the Recover season.)

Fund: You are focused on building savings. Your priority is growing your financial reserves.

Activate: You're spending more freely, using savings for a meaningful purpose, or investing in experiences. Your priority is maximizing the present.

Balance: You are managing both saving and spending, striking a mix between securing your future and enjoying life now. Your priority is maintaining equilibrium.

Based on their calculations, Buck and Penny are in Tier 2 ($50,001 to $150,000) of The Money Target.

TIER 2 INCOME: $50,001 TO $150,000

	Recover	Fund	Activate	Balance
Needs	65%	65%	65%	65%
Wants	10%	12%	25%	19%
Dreams	3%	11%	5%	8%
Fix/Future	20%	7%	3%	4%
Emergency	2%	5%	2%	4%

The Money Target Tier 2 (Buck and Penny's tier). As you saw in chapter 3, these are the percentage allocations organized by season for people whose household income puts them in Tier 2. Choose your percentages for The Money Map based on your tier and your season.

Because Buck and Penny's monthly expenses exceed their income, they are likely racking up debt or depleting savings, if they have them, which is a clear sign they are in the Recover season.

Knowing their season, they transfer the target percentages from the Tier 2, Recover season column into The Money Map under the Target % column.

THE MONEY MAP

	Monthly Total	Actual %	Target %	Adjust
Income	$10,167	N/A	N/A	
Needs	$5,300	52%	65%	
Wants	$1,175	12%	10%	
Dreams	$2,525	25%	3%	
Fixes	$2,300	23%	20%	
Future	$0	0%	0%	
Emergency	$0	0%	2%	
Totals	$11,300	112%	100%	

The Money Map (Buck and Penny, three columns complete). Transfer your target percentages, based on your tier and season from The Money Target. Total target percentages must add up to 100 percent. If not, something was transposed incorrectly. Buck and Penny are in Tier 2, in the Recover season.

Step 3.2: Make the Adjustment

Now we are going to see how far off you are from the target. Amber Dugger, founder of Profit for Keeps, author of *Profit for Joy*, and a coach to thousands on personal budgeting, calls this moment "the awful." The emotional sting you experience when you finally see where your money has been going versus where it needs to go now.

"I always tell clients to leave space after moments of financial truth," she says, "to go for a walk or do something they love. This moment is like ripping off a Band-Aid."

She's right. It's raw. It's real. But it's also the start of real, raw control. Feeling "the awful" means your blindfold is finally off and "the relief" is in sight.

For each category (except INCOME), subtract the number in the Actual % column from the number in the Target % column to calculate the adjustment. Be sure to include a positive (+) or negative (-) sign before the number in the Adjust column to indicate whether you need to increase or decrease spending in that category.

For example, in NEEDS, the target is 65 percent, but Buck and Penny's actual percentage is 52 percent. That means an adjustment of +13 percent, indicating that this category should ideally receive more funding. Now, hold judgment. You might be thinking, *Wait, they need to spend more on NEEDS during the Recover season?* (Answer: In this case, yes.)

Before we act on the numbers, let's finish the full analysis. When we reflect on this process in step 4, we'll reveal real issues in Buck and Penny's spending. For now, run the numbers for each category and complete the Adjust column.

THE MONEY MAP

	Monthly Total	Actual %	Target %	Adjust
Income	$10,167	N/A	N/A	
Needs	$5,300	52%	65%	+13%
Wants	$1,175	12%	10%	-2%
Dreams	$2,525	25%	3%	-22%
Fixes	$2,300	23%	20%	-3%
Future	$0	0%	0%	0%
Emergency	$0	0%	2%	+2%
Totals	$11,300	112%	100%	-12%

The Money Map (Buck and Penny, completed chart). To calculate the Adjust percentages, subtract the Actual % from the Target %, noting the resulting positive or negative percentage.

To verify accuracy, add up all the percentages in the Adjust column. Since some numbers are positive and some are negative, the total should match the difference between your actual percentage total (112%) and your target percentage total (100%).

(+13%) + (-2%) + (-22%) + (-3%) + (0%) + (+2%) = -12%
This matches the difference between 112 percent and 100 percent.

If your numbers align, you've nailed it! If they don't, something might be off. Double-check your calculations.

> ☑ **TAKE QUICK ACTION**
> If this stuff is giving you brain burn (and I get it), just use the free tools at mymoneyhabit.com to do all the work for you.

Step 4.0 Reflect on the Data

Before I share my thoughts, I'm curious about your observations. Take a moment to reflect on these questions:

NEEDS: This category's fix is an increase. Does that surprise you? Could it be that Buck and Penny missed some essential expenses? Looking at the details, is their rent higher than it should be, and are they underspending elsewhere to cover it?

WANTS: This category requires a slight decrease. What do you think? Can they still experience the small luxuries in life? Does it matter to Buck and Penny? Are they simply a victim of living without a budget, forcing them to make a small cut here?

DREAMS: Whoa! This category needs a massive cut. What do you think is causing that? Are big-ticket expenses in this category throwing off the entire budget? Are you blaming Gerg, er, I mean, Buck? 'Cause judgy me kinda is.

FIX: It's odd that this category needs to decrease. Does that seem right? Could this be credit card spending instead of actual debt repayment? Are they just covering minimum payments while continuing to add to their balance? When you see that their FIX category needs a decrease, what emotions come up?

EMERGENCY: With no savings here, does it feel urgent to allocate something? Are they putting themselves at financial risk by not having a safety net? How does it feel to prioritize debt repayment?

Here's what stands out to me when I reflect on this:

NEEDS: Something feels off here. Buck and Penny seem to be living as expected, but where are utilities, health care, and other basic costs? My Spidey sense says something is missing. Rent seems high compared to their income. Would a move make sense? Groceries might also be an area to tighten up.

WANTS: The decrease here is slight, meaning they still have room for everyday enjoyment. I suspect they won't feel the pinch. But a $450/month gym membership? Come on, Penny, you're better than that.

DREAMS: This is the biggest issue, bar none. That luxury car is killing their budget. It's instantly clear that it has to go. Vacations aren't helping either, but maybe they'd be realistic if the luxury car wasn't in the picture. And gifts are nice and all, but are they right and all?

FIX: This part gives me goosebumps, because they actually need to decrease their debt allocations. In other words, they don't need to put as much money to the credit card each month, making the number manageable. But, and it's a big but, the current payments they are making are of little benefit if they continue to swipe. The real solution? Stop using the credit card altogether and aggressively pay down the principal with the allocation suggested. This shift will change everything.

EMERGENCY: This excites me the most. Even setting aside "only" $203 per month (2 percent of monthly income) would build over

$2,000 in savings by year-end. That's a sizeable step toward peace of mind and financial security. And it will only get better over time.

This plan might not always align with what we want to hear, but it delivers what we *need* to hear. With this clarity comes control. Amber Dugger calls this grasp of where you're spending your money "the gateway of awareness." The awareness her Profit for Keeps clients gain about their personal money choices illuminates other truths about relationships, emotional patterns, and even their values. This, in turn, reduces stress and anxiety. Amber says, "You feel more empowered when you understand your financial landscape." I expect you will feel the same when applying The Money Map to your own finances.

If you haven't built your Money Map yet, now's the time. It's fast, easy, and while it might feel a little uncomfortable at first, it will give you the following:

- a clear diagnosis of your financial situation
- a direct path to long-term financial health
- the ability to take control and make informed choices

This is your moment. Your money, your future, and the life you deserve all await. Let's do this now.

Looking at Your Debt

I did not go over debt (or savings) in The Money Map because it's not relevant yet. What is relevant is for us to understand your current cash flow circumstances.

I began investing in businesses as an angel investor about twenty years ago, and I was miserable at it. Less angel investor and more angel of death, if you get my drift. A realization about my repeated failures only came years later. I couldn't fix a single business by trying to fix everything at once. It works only when you focus on one vital need at a time.

When it comes to financial health, we can't fix everything at once either. In fact, there is a specific sequence every financially stressed individual (and business) must follow if they are going to improve their finances. Start with the here and now. You must first fix your current cash flow.

From a financial perspective, if you are losing money every month, it doesn't matter how much debt you have or what you want for the future, your situation is unsustainable. Resolving your finances always follows this sequence:

1 Fix the present day-to-day circumstances first.
2 Then address the past mistakes, in other words debt.
3 Lastly, drive your financial future.

The Money Habit system accounts for all these components from the start but places the necessary focus on current circumstances. And that's why we haven't dived deep into debt yet. While we absolutely must and will address debt completely, it's premature at this moment.

One thing I do want to address are the two common forms of debt, since I refer to them in The Money Target, showing more concern over credit card debt than a mortgage, for example. Here's why.

Asset-Based Debt
This is often called "secured debt" and includes debts like mortgages or car loans, where the item purchased has sustained value and ideally appreciates over time. For example, most homes increase in value over time. Cars, while they typically depreciate, still hold value for a sustained period and can be sold to recover part of their cost.

Liability-Based Debt
This is also referred to as "unsecured debt" and is debt associated with items that have no sustained value or depreciate too quickly to be considered assets. Examples include using credit to buy consumables like food or making purchases like an expensive guitar that

depreciates once used and stored for years. Liability-based debt often shows up on credit card statements, personal loans, and bank loans used for debt consolidation.

While I'm not a fan of debt in general—the emotional weight of it can be overwhelming—differentiating asset-based debt and liability-based debt is crucial. Our focus should be on eliminating liability-based debt first, as it provides no lasting value or benefit. Yet asset-based debt, managed right, can be a huge ally.

Adjusting for Inflation

In the mid-1970s, when I was a corduroy-wearing five-year-old, my mom and I would sit in endless gas lines, waiting for our turn based on a license plate lottery (due to the OPEC oil crisis). It was a time of hyperinflation. So cost cutting was not just with gas.

At home, my parents waged an all-out war on electricity. It was treated like my mom's fine china, always there, never used, reserved strictly to impress guests. The rest of us? We were shamed if we could see our own hands in front of our faces at night. Every room followed a strict one-light-only, last-resort policy, and even that was negotiable.

Carrying a dirty dish from the den? Den light off, kitchen light on just long enough to rinse, then off again. Back to the den, light on, then off once the TV kicked in as our main light source. During commercials? TV off for exactly 120 seconds, like it was powered by gold.

That was inflation survival in the '70s: gas rationing, light-switch gymnastics, and mastering the delicate art of navigating your house by the dying glow of a Zenith TV.

Inflation almost always hits essentials first, meaning the NEEDS account is the priority to address when inflation rises. Food, fuel, and other weekly expenses are affected first, followed by expenses like utilities, transportation (vehicle maintenance, public transportation), and then rent or mortgage rates. This uptick in pricing can happen over months, a year, or years, and it can come in waves. Leases and other contracts hold steady only for as long as they last, so once they expire, inflation catches up with them too.

Since WANTS and DREAMS are non-essential, when inflation hits hard, you can delay or reduce your allocations to them without affecting your daily survival. In the short term, before inflation fully impacts your budget, reducing WANTS and DREAMS and shifting that money to EMERGENCY for six months builds a financial cushion.

Cutting WANTS too aggressively can backfire because it eliminates joy. So find lower-cost alternatives that provide the same mental reward. If a full spa day is out, maybe a group meditation provides a similar sense of relaxation. Avoid making repeated cuts that trigger a sense of loss every time. Instead of going from a spa day to just a massage, then to just a sauna visit, then to meditation, make one big change upfront (spa to meditation) and remove the pain of 1,000 cuts. One big loss is easier to accept than four small ones.

During inflation, if you're renting and your lease ends in twelve months, expect a rent increase and start saving now. A quick search for "How much will rent increase in my area?" will give you a good estimate. If your rent is currently $2,000 per month and expected to increase by 15 percent to $2,300 in six months, start setting aside the extra $300 now in a special NEEDS account dedicated to rent. This forces adjustments in your spending ahead of time and ensures you know whether you can afford the new rent before you renew your lease.

Locking in fixed costs where possible helps stabilize expenses. If you have an adjustable-rate mortgage that resets soon, inflation could drive up payments significantly. A fixed-rate mortgage is usually safer. If rates drop, you can refinance, but if they rise, you're already locked in at a lower rate.

Inflation requires quick, proactive adjustments. Secure essentials first, shift money toward stability, and reduce financial shocks by preparing for future costs today.

Money Shame Can Be a Catalyst for Change

Money shame is normal, but not necessary. Many of us have felt the sting of embarrassment when facing financial difficulties, and I'm no exception.

Years ago, my family went on vacation with close friends. It was a trip we couldn't afford, and my friend Chris covered the entire bill for my family. While I was deeply grateful for his generosity, I was also overwhelmed with shame. I felt inadequate for not being able to provide for my family. That moment stuck with me, not just because of the financial strain, but because I realized how my money mismanagement had stolen my confidence. However, I also discovered that shame, while painful, could be a catalyst for change.

If you're feeling money shame, know that this is your moment to choose differently. The best way to overcome shame is to act. Start by acknowledging your current reality without judgment. Then, commit to mastering your finances one step at a time. The Money Habit system offers a simple and actionable framework to guide you. By taking control, you're not just managing money, you're reclaiming your confidence and your future.

When I put this system in place, I didn't become rich overnight. Neither will you. But I did gain something far more powerful: confidence. From day one, I felt more in control. Within months, I saw meaningful progress. There were slip-ups along the way, but I always returned to the system and stayed the course.

If you haven't yet, finish The Money Map and build your action plan. You'll gain clarity, control, and confidence in your financial journey. This is your moment to transform your relationship with money and move forward with purpose.

GET 'ER DONE SUMMARY
BUILD YOUR MONEY MAP.

1. **Calculate your monthly usable income (MUI).** Tally all net income coming into your household and divide by 12. This is your usable income, after taxes and deductions.

2. **Track your spending.** Review recent statements and categorize every expense into NEEDS, WANTS, DREAMS, FIX, FUTURE, or EMERGENCY. Don't worry about perfection; ballpark estimates are fine.

3. **Compare your actuals to The Money Target.** Use your current tier and financial season to find your Money Target percentages. Then compare what you're currently spending to where the money *should* be going.

4. **Calculate your gaps and realign.** Where are you overspending or under-allocating? What needs immediate correction? This is the moment of truth. Don't judge yourself. The goal isn't guilt; it's clarity.

5

Gain Control with Clarity Accounts

A VISION BOARD dream fulfilled. And all it took was one offhand comment, ten years, and about seventy-five bucks.

Okay, actually, seventy-five bucks squirreled away monthly in a secret account, but who's counting?

In 2008, I hit my financial rock bottom. But, after using the Money Habit system, by 2013, I had my debt fully under control. I was still in my Recover season, but I had paid off all my active credit cards and the system I followed (which I will share with you in the next chapter) ensured I would put all my debt to rest within a few years.

On New Year's Eve in 2013, Krista and I sat down to create our vision board for 2014, a ritual we had been doing for a few years. We would cut out pictures and phrases from magazines that represented experiences we wanted in the new year and paste them onto a poster board. Financial recovery can make it easy to forget to dream, and even easier to lose sight of what excites your partner or brings them happiness. On the surface, it was just a craft project. Cutting, gluing, and arranging images. But emotionally, it was a small way to keep our dreams alive and to bring a little hope and enthusiasm to the road of financial recovery still ahead of us.

It always surprises me that many of the things we paste onto vision boards actually come about. Maybe not immediately or in that year, but sure enough they happen more often than not. I don't think vision boards are anything magical; they work because the ritual brings the things we want into conscious thought and then we can act on them. Even if the action is itsy-bitsy.

That year, Krista pasted a picture of Canyon Ranch on our 2014 board. I'd never heard of it, so I asked her about it.

"It's my dream self-care retreat," she said. "It's a resort I saw mentioned on *The Oprah Winfrey Show* as the best of the best for wellness. You can learn about nutrition, eat healthy gourmet meals, get massages, exercise with trainers. It's basically a health nut's resort with a boatload of pampering."

As she described Canyon Ranch, I could see how much it meant to her, so after we finished our vision board, I looked it up. Holy wow, that place was expensive. Like $5,000 for two people for three days expensive. *My God*, I thought. *Who can afford that? I guess, Oprah.*

And then I thought, *Why not open an account and see what happens?*

Since we were still in the Recover season, I determined we could put seventy-five dollars away each month toward it and still finish off the debt within our timeline. I went full incognito, since I didn't want to tip off Krista. I set up an account and labeled it D-CRT (my code for DREAM-Canyon Ranch Trip) and an automatic transfer. Then I used a "hide" feature in our online banking so Krista wouldn't stumble upon it.* I also did that so I would forget about it. Which I did!

The seventy-five-dollar transfer happened each month and I didn't even notice. I forgot about the account, and I forgot about

---

* The bank you are considering may not offer features that will help, like hiding accounts until you want to see them. So go to mymoneyhabit.com to see the best banks.

the trip. Every so often when I went through bank statements, I would see the D-CRT account sitting there. I would look at the balance, and I was always surprised. I remember peeking at the account a few years after setting it up and it had passed $2,000. A few years later, it neared that $5,000 goal I had set. But life went on and I didn't pay much attention to it; at one point I even forgot what that old D-CRT stood for.

Then, near the end of 2023, a friend of mine mentioned that she went on a women's retreat and stayed at "the fabled Canyon Ranch" for a few days. She went on to explain how the all-inclusive wellness retreat was like no other. *Canyon Ranch? Oh, yeah, Canyon Ranch! D-CRT!!!* Fired up, I logged into the account, and we had over $8,000 in there. That's when I booked the trip.

That Christmas, I told Krista I had a surprise getaway for her in 2024. I gave her the dates and told her I would give her the details one week before we left so she could pack accordingly. On September 18, 2024, while we were visiting my college buddy Matt Cox, I told her, "We are going to Canyon Ranch next week."

Tears streamed down her face, and she started shaking. And then I got the biggest hug of my life from her. Matt's my witness.

The trip cost a little more than $5,000; inflation happens over ten years. But the $9,000 I had saved by the time we left on the trip, at seventy-five bucks a month, was more than enough. We went for a four-day trip, and we had a little over $1,000 extra she could use to buy some cool outfits, Canyon Ranch swag, *and* get a massage treatment when she got back from a weekend away of getting massages. The best part? I didn't worry about spending a single dime of it. I was there for every moment physically, mentally, and emotionally.

Krista and I still do our annual vision board ritual. Now, though, I realize opening a Money Habit clarity account is the ultimate form of financial manifestation. It doesn't matter if its seventy-five dollars or one dollar. By setting money aside to fund something specific, you are acting on your dreams. You are letting the universe, and your subconscious, know your dreams are more than desires; they are intentions.

The Power of Clarity Accounts

In chapter 3, I introduced you to Sam. After his husband passed away, he found himself in a financial crisis that seemed impossible to resolve. Once we got a handle on his situation, we were ready to allocate his income to accounts. Because he tended to forget how much he would need for each bill, Sam needed more specificity than the six foundational accounts provide. So we added a few clarity accounts.

In the Recover season, NEEDS and FIX are the essentials, so I asked Sam: What are your "essential essentials" that you worry about most? For Sam, those were food, shelter, and heat. So, within the NEEDS category, we added a few accounts and gave them prefixes to identify their categories. We also added one WANT account to satisfy his inner rebel and give him hope. Sam's Recover season accounts looked like this:

- N-Groceries—Food and supplies for his apartment. N, since they are an essential need.

- N-Rent—Shelter is an N.

- N-Heat—Heat (gas) and electricity. Also essential, so N.

- F-Citi Credit Card—This was to tackle his one credit card with outstanding debt. It gets an F since it is a FIX. Not to be confused with F for FUTURE, so for further clarity you could spell out the entirety of FIX or FUTURE as the prefix. And as Sam puts it, he kinda likes the idea of "F Citi," if you catch his drift. *Ba dum tss.*

- W-Small Joys—For tiny indulgences to keep deprivation burnout at bay. W for WANT.

Now, when Sam logged into his accounts, he instantly saw what money was available for what purpose. If his N-Groceries account ran low, he'd know he had to either adjust his funding by working overtime or rethink how he was allocating money elsewhere.

This granular level of detail gave Sam the confidence to manage his money instead of feeling like it was managing him.

But clarity is more than categories; it's meaningful categories. So we made sure Sam's account names worked for him specifically. N-Rent and N-Groceries were straightforward and meaningful, but W-Small Joys? That sounded dull to him. He got excited when we renamed it W-Girl, Just Do It, and for taxes, he loved calling his FIX account F-The Gubber-ment (Sam apparently likes *F* jokes as much as I do). For the N-Heat account, he leaned toward N-This Beeyotch Gotta Stay Warm. To each their own, I suppose. Personalize your accounts to make them both functional and engaging.

Sam's story is still playing out while you are reading this book. He likely has years of transformation in front of him. But, within minutes, he had financial clarity like never before. He managed to work things out with his landlords and keep paying his bills. Surely he will slip up as he journeys forward; we're only human after all. But the power of the Money Habit system is that once you see the financial clarity, right there at your bank, you will never unsee it. And those mistakes? No worries, my friend, the system takes care of those too.

These specialized clarity accounts work alongside your foundational accounts to take the guesswork out of your finances. They provide hyper-specific visibility into the expenses you think (or worry) about most. These accounts are specific-use accounts that break down your existing NEEDS, WANTS, DREAMS, FIX/FUTURE, and EMERGENCY accounts into clearer, more precise categories.

Your NEEDS account already covers essentials like housing, food, transportation, and so on. But what if every trip to the grocery store still feels like rolling the dice? What if you want more granular insight into what money you have for what purchases? Instead of lumping all expenses into one broad NEED category, you can create clarity accounts for specific areas of spending that cause you stress.

For example, instead of a single NEEDS account, you might set up the following:

- N-Groceries (to track food expenses separately)
- N-Rent (so you always know your rent is covered)
- N-Gas (for your car's fuel expenses)

Now, instead of constantly wondering if you can afford groceries or panicking about rent, you see the exact amount sitting in your account without mental math or guesswork.

And it doesn't stop at NEEDS. You can apply the same approach with your WANTS, DREAMS, FIX/FUTURE, and EMERGENCY accounts:

- W-Dining Out (for guilt-free restaurant splurges)
- F-Personal Loan Payback (for finally squaring up with your buddy who covered you during tight times)
- W-Hobbies (for things like books, video games, music lessons—yes, the guitar obsession counts)
- D-Vacation Fund (for that dream trip you've been mentally packing for, for the last five years)
- E-The Pooch (for when you rush your dog to the vet after he eats an entire roast chicken, bones and all *#TrueStory*)

These accounts don't have to be permanent. Once a goal has been achieved or a specific stressor is no longer an issue, you can roll the balance back into the respective foundational account or rename it for your next financial goal. For example, when I finally buy that D-New Guitar, I will rename the account to D-Yet Another New Guitar because I am always one broken string away from an irresistible excuse to get another.

When you can see exactly how much you have for a specific expense, two things happen:

1. Your stress levels drop because you're not second-guessing whether you have enough.
2. You make better financial decisions. You eradicate overextending yourself or overspending in one area at the expense of another.

If you're picturing a nightmare scenario where your bank app is flooded with endless accounts, that's not how this works. Most people find they need only five or so clarity accounts, in addition to their foundational accounts, at any given time, and the accounts evolve over time. When starting out, you may need only one or two clarity accounts to target the biggest sources of financial stress. That alone can be a game changer.

More accounts are helpful only if they bring clarity and reduce stress. If they start feeling like financial clutter, it's time to ratchet down.

Setting up clarity accounts allows you to control your money as you see fit, not based on what an "expert" or budget template tells you to do. Lack of autonomy and control over your finances is a big reason why budgets fail. As Amber Dugger, the budgeting expert you met in chapter 4, puts it: "Templates are loaded with implied judgment." She warns that tools like budgeting apps often come with default categories and values that mess with your mindset. "People see tithing, daycare, or charity in there, and if they don't have that category in their life, they start to feel like they're doing money wrong." That's why the Money Habit system doesn't tell you what to value; it gives you the structure to support *what you already value.*

THE POWER OF CLARITY ACCOUNTS

Account Number	Account Name	Balance
*2000	Income	$0
*3001	N-Mortgage	$3,575
*3002	W-Krista's Debit	$800
*4001	W-Mike's Debit	$35
*4002	W-Date Days	$190
*4003	D-LBI House	$38,000
*4004	F-Stock Market	$18,000

The power of clarity accounts. Here's a peek at some of the accounts my wife and I use. This is how they show up when we log into our bank app. Personalized, purposeful, and crystal clear.

This is a snapshot of some of our clarity accounts. Krista and I can instantly see what money is available for what purpose, and so can you. That's the beauty of this system.

Let's do a quick test. Imagine it's the middle of the month and we're checking these bank accounts to make money decisions.

First up: the INCOME account. It's sitting at zero. That means everything from the last paycheck has already been allocated. One more paycheck is coming in this month, and when it does, it'll get distributed too. Now let me ask you a few questions.

Our mortgage is $5,000 a month. Can we pay it today?

Nope. The Mortgage account only has $3,575 in it. But since we do this regularly, I know the next paycheck's allocation will cover the rest.

Krista wants to take a friend out for lunch and pick up the tab. Can she?

Yep! Her W-Krista's Debit account has $800 in it. As long as she's not heading to some off-the-charts-expensive place, she's good.

How about me? Can I take my buddy out for lunch?

Maybe. But only if we're hitting a local deli. I've got $35 in my W-Mike's Debit account. I also have to consider what I won't be able to get if I use that money. Like, two lunches for myself.

Krista and I want to go out on a date tonight. What are we doing?

Whatever adds up to less than $190, because that's what's in our W-Date Days account. That might mean a movie and dinner or just ice cream and a walk, which would mean cash left for another date. I like option two!

Now check out our F-Stock Market account. We've got $18,000 saved there. I could invest that. Or, if the market's dipping, I might just sit on the cash and wait.

And then there's the D-LBI House account. We've got $38,000 set aside toward our beach house dream. It's a solid start, but every time I browse real estate apps, I'm reminded just how far we still have to go. Apparently, they aren't giving away bayfront properties "down the shore."

Here's the point: I know exactly what each dollar is for. So does Krista. So do you. You just had seconds of exposure to my finances, yet you mastered it. There's no guessing, no stress. Just clarity.

Once you have the basic Money Habit system down, use clarity accounts to customize it however you like to suit your daily life, to alleviate the stress of ambiguity, and to fund your dreams. Maybe you want more than one EMERGENCY fund: maybe one for unexpected house repairs and another for health care. Maybe you want to take multiple fancy trips. Maybe you simply want to get more specific about expenses. You have control. This is *your* system to tweak however you see fit. It's important to me that you get that, because when you set up the accounts that matter to you, you are more likely to follow the system.

Make It Your Own

What if "one day" could become a specific day? What if you stopped questioning whether your dream can happen, and instead determined the moment it will happen? What if you stopped wondering *if* and started expecting *when*?

Justin Stafford isn't saving for a "someday" trip. The Money Habit system enables him to determine exactly *when* he can take the trip, so someday becomes a specific day on the calendar. "I was always frustrated with myself because I didn't have enough money to do what I wanted to do," Justin said in an interview for this book.

"Me and my buddy had been talking about going out to Alaska. We have a friend who charters fishing trips, so all we'd need to worry about paying for was the plane ticket there and back. But I never really had the opportunity to say, 'Yeah, I can definitely save the money by this date.' I couldn't commit to the plan, because I always had to cover something else. Now, I actually have that ability. Based on my new money management abilities, I can basically figure out to the date when my buddy and I are going to be able to make that trip."

Justin joined the Money Habit program at A1 Garage Door Service because he wanted to learn how to control his finances. "I had started making a lot more money than I was used to," he explained, "but I was still stuck in my old ways, spending whatever money was in my account. My net worth was basically whatever paycheck I got that week."

Getting out of the old money cycle was his top priority. Instead of worrying about how he would cover his bills each month, or if he would be able to handle unexpected expenses, he wanted to know for sure he had enough.

Justin is in the Fund season, working toward having four months of living expenses saved up, a new (to him) truck with the upgrades he wants, the Alaska trip, and most important on his list: his seven-year-old daughter's future. "Lillian is my whole world,"

Justin said. "When she's old enough to have the kind of needs I have, I want her to have a cushion. If she decides to buy a house at eighteen, she'll have a little bit of money on top of whatever else she saved up. Or, if she wants to get a new car."

A house at eighteen? I could barely afford my used Nissan to get to college and back. Great dad there, Lillian. You're a lucky kid.

Once he had a handle on the Money Habit system, Justin adjusted the accounts to work for his everyday life, his goals, and his habits. Before his paycheck hits his account, he already has several "out of sight, out of mind" withdrawals: child support for his daughter, health insurance, and his 401(k). Once the net pay hits his INCOME account, he transfers funds to five accounts. Here's the breakdown:

N-Rent: This is Justin's savings account for his monthly rent, and anything related to running his house, such as utilities and internet. The bills are on auto-pay, except for his rent. To ensure he doesn't spend any of the money in this account, he doesn't keep a checkbook. Instead, he drives to the bank once a month and gets a cashier's check for rent and drops it off at his landlord's house. "I figured out how much I need each week to cover everything I need to run the house, and after I transfer that amount to my N-Rent account, I divide the rest of my income into the five accounts, *including* the N-Rent account. That way, if I don't work for a week, I still have money in that account, and everything is covered."

In this way, Justin's N-Rent account is doing double-duty as his EMERGENCY account. Once he has four months of living expenses saved in his N-Rent account, thanks to the weekly overage, he will stop putting extra money into that account. This way, in case of an emergency, he has rent already secured for four months. And he knew the exact date on which he would hit that goal. Specifically, eight months after starting the Money Habit program.

WANTS: This is a personal savings account that's easier to access than Justin's other savings accounts. He uses this account if he needs a new pair of boots, for example.

DREAMS: This is a personal savings account Justin uses to save for a new truck and his planned vacations, like his Alaska trip.

F-Lillian's Future: This is a personal savings account for Lillian's future needs, wants, or dreams.

W-General Spending: What's left he uses for general spending, "everyday stuff I need for work and whatnot; my drinks, cigarettes, maybe a lunch or something like that." He tries to limit the money in the General Spending account to $250 per week. (I would prefer he keep that account at zero, after disbursements to the other accounts, but it works for him.) He keeps this at his existing bank for ease of access. The other four accounts are all at a different bank where he gets a better interest rate.

The Money Habit program taught Justin to think about how he is naturally wired, which helped him realize that every time he spent his full weekly paycheck in a week, he was falling into the trap of Parkinson's Law.

New to Parkinson's Law? It is a behavioral principle that translates to your expenses rise to match your income. In other words, the more money you see sitting in your account, the more you unconsciously find ways to spend it. It's not a character flaw; it's wiring. Justin didn't try to out-discipline Parkinson's Law, nor should you. Instead, design around this spend-it-all tendency by making some of your money inaccessible.

"I'm a major out of sight, out of mind kind of a guy," Justin explained. "When I open my bank account on my phone and see the available funds, I think I can spend all that right now. So, I keep all my accounts except my General Spending account completely separate, in a different bank. And I don't have that bank's app on my phone. If I want to mess with any of those accounts, I have to physically go down to the bank." Rather than try to force himself to change that habit, he went all in on the out of sight, out of mind component of the Money Habit system.

Five accounts designed for clarity. Pretty simple, and it works for Justin. "It makes me feel more comfortable knowing that my money's going to be available when I need it. I know one hundred percent of my bills will be paid. I have no worries or stress about money whatsoever."

There it is! This is the reason I hope you do this, and the reason I wrote this book for you. *I have no worries or stress about money whatsoever.* I want you to feel that too. You will be forever grateful to yourself, and your Lillian, if you have one, will be to you too.

Eventually, Justin will start saving for a down payment on a house. But right now, he's taking his time. "I was the epitome of an impulse buyer before The Money Habit," he said. "That's what led me to purchase my first house, which put me in a bind. I don't want to be in that situation again, so I'm giving the whole money management system a solid year to get used to it, to get it really dialed in, and then I'll set a date for when I want to have a down payment for a house." Once he has that date, like with the Alaska trip, he'll figure out how much he needs to set aside for the down payment, open a clarity account, and calculate new allocations.

The Money Habit isn't a rigid system. Yes, there are guiding principles and essential functions that need to be in place, but it's designed to flex with your tendencies. If you need to hide accounts to protect yourself from yourself, do it. If piling up a buffer in your Rent account works better than having a separate EMERGENCY account, then do that for now. If calling it General Spending feels better than labeling it WANTS, that's perfect. This system is about working with your wiring, not against it. Do what feels right, but just skip those cigarettes. You too, Justin.

You can customize the Money Habit system to fit your needs and goals, then adapt it again as those needs and goals evolve. Do what is intuitive for you and works seamlessly with the way you operate. The Money Habit isn't about a one-size-fits-all or global best practice approach to money management. It's about aligning with your habits, not mine or anyone else's, to maximize your mastery of money.

Understanding NEEDS vs. WANTS

One of the most common questions I get from people learning to use the Money Habit system is, "How do I figure out if an expense is a need or a want?" On the surface, the answer may seem obvious, but as you start using the system, you'll run into the nuance of that question. For example, one couple couldn't decide if the monthly fee for their gym was a NEED or a WANT. On the surface, gym fees are a WANT. We can all get exercise without paying for it. Except the gym had free childcare, which is a big deal when you have three kids. This couple used the gym's day care several times a week, because it was the only time they could get a break to run errands and handle other adult responsibilities. So was the gym a NEED or a WANT? Good question. I'd like to think they could find alternative childcare options, such as trading with other parents or leaning on family, but what if they didn't have those options?

Ultimately, you get to decide if an expense is a NEED or a WANT. Here's a guide to help you figure that out:

- NEEDS are the essentials for life. See them as the *bare minimum*. They are the things required for survival and stability. You must eat and drink, you must have shelter, basic transportation, clothing, health care, and so on.

- WANTS are the enhancements and upgrades to life. See them as the *betterments*. These improve the quality of life but are not necessary for functioning.

A good litmus test: If you cut it out completely, would your health, safety, or ability to work and function suffer? If yes, it's a NEED. If no, it's a WANT.

You could also consider WANTS as NEEDS that are "upgraded." Groceries (NEEDS) vs. dining out (WANTS). Transportation (NEED) vs. a luxury SUV (WANT or DREAM). Determining the difference is not about deprivation but about intentional choices. Be *very* careful about the human nature to justify—to say that a WANT (my fancy pickup truck) is really a NEED (a beater car). I justify the truck because I "need" to go to Home Depot to get things like the new grill that I "need" and can only get it home with the truck I "need." These are wants.

NEEDS VS. WANTS

Category	Needs	Wants
Food	Groceries, basic meals	Dining out, premium ingredients, coffee shop drinks
Housing	Rent, mortgage, utilities	Larger home, extra amenities, home decor upgrades
Transportation	Basic car, public transit	Newer car, rideshares, convenience upgrades
Clothing	Weather-appropriate basics	Designer brands, trendy items, accessories
Health	Insurance, essential care	Spa treatments, elective procedures
Entertainment	Free or low-cost activities	Streaming services, concerts, vacations

NEEDS VS. WANTS. NEEDS are the essential and necessities for living. WANTS are the small or big betterments, upgrades, or extras.

The Evolution of My Accounts

The Money Habit works at all different income levels. I can speak to this, since I have used it in a year when I made $9,699 (that is the exact amount I earned in 2008 when I started this system). The only time I made less was when I worked part time in college in the early '90s earning about $3,500 each year. I have used this system when making $100,000 or thereabouts for over a decade and used it when making $750,000 and more. It worked every time. And it has served me just as effectively at every level. The system is adaptable. And awareness and control happen at every level.

Let's be real: My finances today don't look like they did fifteen years ago, or even five years ago. Yours will likely change too. Perhaps dramatically. Hopefully for the better and better. But the reality is it could tank too. Here's a snapshot of what my Money Habit accounts looked like at three distinct financial seasons of my life.

My Recover Season ($75,000/Year)

Back when our household income was about $75,000 per year, we had a house and three children, leaving us very little wiggle room in our budget. Day-to-day cash clarity meant more than ever at this point. Plus, we had debt we needed to fix, putting us squarely in the Recover season.

MIKE'S ACCOUNTS (TIER 2 INCOME)

Account	Deposits	Notes
Income	$1,442	Weekly paycheck after taxes
N-Mortgage	$400	Covers $1,600 mortgage
N-Groceries	$150	No dining out—strict grocery budget
N-Utilities	$75	Bare necessities
W-Family Fun	$25	Pizza night or a cheap movie rental
E-Emergency Fund	$50	Protecting against emergencies
F-Retirement	$50	Small, but building future security

Mike's accounts/Tier 2 income. This is a sampling of accounts I had during my Recover season. Note that F-Retirement is a clarity account under the FUTURE category. I was crushing debt (that account is not shown here), but I had a tax deferred investment account, through work, where it made financial sense to save for the future while prioritizing the fix of my past.

Important note: Since this table displays only a sample of my accounts, the percentages for each category may not perfectly align with the recommendations for the Recover season.

I couldn't fund big dreams yet, but I had clarity and peace of mind. The system protected me from going deeper into debt.

My Fund Season ($250,000/Year)

Years later, I had created a business that brought in a steady flow of big projects and my financial situation significantly improved. This initiated a big jump in my company's income *and* mine. And at about $250,000 annually, Krista and I felt more comfortable, yet valued the intentionality behind the system even more. We shifted to the Fund season, preparing for future events like vacations, education, and retirement. At the same time, we chose to get out for more frequent date nights. Even though the Fund stage concentrates less on WANTS, since The Money Targets are percentage based, the increased income freed up more of the "fun" in Fund.

MIKE'S ACCOUNTS (TIER 3 INCOME)

Account	Deposits	Notes
Income	$3,125	Weekly paycheck after taxes
N-Mortgage	$1,100	Overpaying installments
N-Groceries	$200	Room for healthier choices
W-Dining & Date Nights	$150	Occasional nicer dinners
D-Family Vacation	$100	Annual trip became possible
D-Kids' Education	$150	Increased savings for college
F-Retirement	$250	Building meaningful security

Sample of Mike's accounts/Tier 3 income. The example of my accounts during a FUND season shows an increased savings orientation, overpaying the mortgage to get it down faster and saving for future events. The increased income allowed us to boost grocery costs for healthier food and dates out for a healthier marriage.

Now there was space for WANTS and DREAMS, but I still couldn't splurge without thought. Each account brought clarity and eliminated overspending temptation.

My Life Today, the Balance Season

Today, my income is significantly higher. It took decades to get here, and it could still go somewhere else. Like you, if my income is going to move, I want it to go up, up, and up. But life happens: layoffs, recessions, curveballs, and in an instant, it can drop to zero. In fact, my income has gone back to zero four separate times in my adult life.

We just wrapped up an Activate season, using wedding funds (as you know), taking a few epic trips, and renovating the house maybe a bit too much. It got to the point where the neighbors started asking if we'd ever have a week without contractors. Apparently hammers and circular saws are loud. But it was all part of the plan, all within the season. Now, we're shifting into Balance (and quiet in the neighborhood).

MIKE'S ACCOUNTS (TODAY)

Account	Deposits	Notes
Income	Weekly	Fully allocated
N-Mortgage & Buffer	$1,450	Extra principal plus security
N-Groceries & Health	$400	Higher quality food and wellness
W-Krista's Debit	$200	Krista's personal spending
W-Mike's Debit	$75	My personal entertainment
W-Date Days	$150	Consistent special experiences
D-Family Vacation	$500	Larger or multiple family trips
D-Kids' Weddings	$196	Now practical and doable
F-Investments	$350	Significant weekly investment
N-Taxes	$1,680	Necessary evil
N-Health Emergencies	$250	Health emergencies

Sample of Mike's accounts today. As my wife and I shift into the Balance season, we are focusing on saving for dreams while spending on experiences we want to become treasured memories.

At this stage, dreams are bigger, yet clarity remains critical. The core practice, allocating every dollar, never changes. The scale and specifics evolve, but the habit remains constant.

Clarity Accounts to Tackle Financial Uncertainty

As your circumstances or goals change, you may want to add clarity accounts to manage specific problems. I'm a total geek for this stuff, so I have quite a few such accounts: one to save for replacing my roof in the future (sorry, neighbors), which is separate from the ongoing home repair account. Creating these is not a must, but they can be helpful at times. Here are a few scenarios and how to use clarity accounts to navigate financial uncertainty.

The Grocery Fix

Grocery costs are creeping up, making it harder to stay within budget. Instead of using a credit card, shift more into an N-Groceries account to absorb the increase; planning meals and cutting impulse buys also keep the budget in check. Doing this will force you to reconsider the other accounts. Maybe we need to trim on the WANTS and DREAMS to balance back out. Or maybe it is time for a side hustle. No matter what, by adjusting, you are now proactively thinking of your next move. Well done!

> ☑ **TAKE QUICK ACTION**
> Use a debit card for groceries. When everyday expenses keep landing on a credit card, it's harder to break an overspending cycle. Using a debit card linked to the N-Groceries account weekly ensures essentials are covered in cash and that you don't buy those tempting extra things, since the money is not there.

The Health Hike Buffer

You're six months out from that time of year no one looks forward to: health insurance open enrollment. And with it comes the annual surprise of new pricing. You know it will happen; you just don't know how much your premium will jump from *ridiculous* to *ridonkulous*. Start socking money into an N-Medical Premium account now, giving yourself a six-month runway. When the new premium hits, your cash flow is already adjusted. And if, by some miracle, it stays relatively flat? Sweet relief! Redirect that buffer into your W-Wellness account and finally enjoy that long-overdue *you* day.

The Side Hustle to Fix That Annoying Thing

Maybe you want to whack out that one stinking credit card balance once and for all. And you side-hustle to do it. In that case, use all the extra cash from the hustle to pay off the credit card, in an F-Credit Card Debt account. Get it done. Then, if you keep the side hustle, make the extra cash into a life boost where you disburse the income through your current Money Map without changing the percentages.

The Car Repair Cushion

The car starts making a weird noise, and instead of panicking, you check the N-Home and Car Maintenance account and see that money has already been set aside for this exact situation. No need to put it on a credit card or scramble for cash. Or maybe you have a D-New Car account, and it is the only one with available money. Now you face the decision: Is it worth repairing the car and holding on longer or do you want (and have enough) to go new? Not enough now, you pull from D-New Car to pay for the old car's repair, knowing that the DREAM of the new car will be delayed some, but the repaired old car is giving you a lot more time to save for the new one. So you feel good.

The Subscription Audit

Subscription services have stacked up, and the monthly bill is getting absurd. These are WANTS. You move all subscriptions to one card, and my G you are spending a lot. So you decide to binge and cut: You devote a weekend to binge all the shows you can imagine on one streaming channel and then cancel the channel. You do this each weekend, and after a month you have canceled four streaming channels and are saving over one hundred dollars a month. That now gets directed to EMERGENCY instead of WANTS. And within a year you have a nice cushion in your emergency fund.

The Try It First Rule

A major lifestyle upgrade, like buying a new home or a new car, looks tempting. Before you make the leap, moving the expected increased cost into a mock account for six months proves whether the new purchase is actually affordable. So you make a W-Car Payment account, and you start paying for it by putting the money in and seeing how this affects other parts of your life. If you can keep it up for six months, you are good, *plus* you have a cushion of money for the car payments. If you can't manage, it just isn't time yet.

> **☑ TAKE QUICK ACTION**
>
> A great technique to manage spending is to look at a clarity account immediately before you go into a store (whether brick and mortar or online). Use your debit card and check the account balance immediately after the purchase. Seeing how much is there, and then how much leaves, keeps you in control.

Here's How You Could Screw This Up

In the early days of developing the Money Habit system, I made a lot of mistakes. Heck, I still make mistakes. And I've watched early adopters of the system make mistakes. Fortunately, you can learn from our blunders to ensure it doesn't happen to you. Here's what to watch out for as you deploy The Money Habit in your life.

Overcomplication

I've seen it happen that someone sets up way too many accounts, thinking they're being hyper-organized, only to drown in the details. A Grocery account? Sure. But add a Bathroom Products account and a Fresh Fruit account, and suddenly, you've created chaos. Too many accounts dilute clarity, and without it, the whole system can collapse. The key? Stick to the core accounts (NEEDS, WANTS, DREAMS, etc.) and only add more when it truly boosts motivation or clarity.

Being Too Logical

This system isn't just about numbers; it's about behavior. And behavior is deeply tied to emotion. A Taxes account might seem logical, but it doesn't tell your brain what it's for. Is it for property taxes? Income taxes? It's too vague. Instead, use emotionally charged names. For example, "CRT" (Canyon Ranch Trip) inspires excitement, while "The Feds' Tax Money" reminds you not to touch it. Emotional triggers keep you on track and engaged.

Neglecting or Forgetting Accounts

Even seasoned Money Habit enthusiasts (like me) aren't immune to this. I've accidentally pulled from the wrong account because I forgot another one existed. For instance, I dipped into our car fund when I should've used the kids' car account. It caused confusion and extra juggling. To avoid this, regularly review your accounts. It's better to be intentional than reactive.

Paralysis by Analysis

The beauty of this system is simplicity. Don't ruin it by overthinking. The Money Habit isn't about tracking every penny; it's about crushing the dollars.

My mom is a perfect example of what *not* to do: She reconciles her checkbook monthly, spending hours (sometimes days) to track down discrepancies of a few pennies. If she's off by just literal cents, she'll make calls (to her "handsome, young" son), visit the bank, and dig into every detail until she figures it out. Over the past sixty years, she and my dad caught the bank making exactly one mistake. One. Back in the '70s, a fifty-dollar deposit wasn't processed. She still fears they'll make another mistake.

Now, I'm not suggesting you ignore accuracy or reconciling, but that level of detail can be overwhelming for some people (me, for example). It can lead to frustration and ultimately giving up, and *that* would be the bigger mistake. With The Money Habit, your money is pre-categorized for you, so you can intuitively spot when something seems off and investigate without all the painstaking detail.

You Already Have a (Somewhat) Working System

If you've got routines or approaches that are already working for you, don't toss them out like fries at the bottom of the bag. This isn't an all-or-nothing deal. Instead, think of The Money Habit as a toolkit. Pick and choose the elements that enhance what you're already doing. The goal isn't to overhaul your approaches for the sake of change; it's to make it even better.

False Sense of Security

Setting up the system is just the start. It's not a "set it and forget it" deal. We still have some setting to do. I've seen people shocked by an unexpected tax bill because they weren't reviewing and adjusting regularly. Quarterly check-ins are crucial to stay on track and avoid nasty surprises.

Blaming the System

This one's a trap. The Money Habit forces hard decisions upfront, because it's supposed to. But when people hit a roadblock ("I can't afford this because my account is empty"), they sometimes blame the system instead of themselves. They abandon it entirely, convinced that no system works. The system doesn't break your finances; it reveals what is already broken. Stick with it, and the rewards will come.

Spending Can Be Pain Free

On day two of our trip to Canyon Ranch in Arizona, Krista and I got up around six to hike the trail that surrounds the facility and watch the sun rise. We walked to the top of a ridge with coffees that were prepared for us by resort staff. We stood in the fresh air, listening to the birds beginning their day. The sun just started to peak into the valley and light flooded the area.

As we took it all in, a small herd of javelina (they look like wild pigs) walked across the path about a hundred yards from us. The sun cast a shadow from the massive trees, and it seemed like a moment from *The Lion King*.

Krista teared up said, "This is heaven."

Yes, it kinda is.

Even though I created it, the effectiveness of the Money Habit system still amazes me. Not only is saving pain reduced but spending is pain free. Because I set up a custom D-CRT account, I didn't need to do the "I could make this happen if I don't pay for this other thing" dance. The funds were there, ready to go. I didn't have to say *someday* and instead picked *the* day.

I know it is bold to say being free of financial worry is heaven. But it kinda is.

Another experience on the vision board checked off.

GET 'ER DONE SUMMARY
MAKE THE DREAM A COMMITMENT.
AND A COMMITMENT BECOMES REALITY.

1. **Pick your dream.** Choose one thing, big or small, that lights you up. If nothing jumps to mind, think about what would bring someone you love joy.

2. **Open a new account.** Log into your bank and open a new savings account. Label it with your dream: D-Canyon Ranch, D-New Guitar, D-Surprise Trip, whatever it is. Make it specific, personal, and fun. The label is the nudge.

3. **Automate a transfer.** Set up an automatic transfer on a dollar or percentage basis. Seventy-five dollars, twenty-five dollars, even five dollars a week. Whatever you can spare. Just set it and forget it.

4. **Hide the account.** If you raid it, you erase it. Use your bank's hide feature or move the account to a separate bank. Out of sight really does reduce temptation.

5. **Celebrate when you check it.** Peek in occasionally. That balance is the physical proof that your dream is in motion. It's happening, baby. It's really happening!

6

Crush Your Debt

AT DOM ANDERSON'S house, unopened bills stacked up like a monument to a dying dream.

"I was scared of money," Dom told me. "The idea of handling my finances was overwhelming to me. Anytime I had to deal with my credit score, or bill collectors, I avoided it." Each envelope served as a silent accusation of failure.

When Dom started earning a higher salary at A1 Garage Door Service, he knew it could go one of two ways: blow through the extra money with nothing to show for it or use it to get closer to his goals. He joined the Money Habit program because he wanted the second path.

His dream was to start a private equity company and invest in properties. But that dream seemed to be off in the distance, way off. First, he had to get a handle on his money and his debt.

"I wanted to be in the '800 club,' as in my credit score," Dom said. "It seemed so unattainable. I had a credit score of 530. How could I get to 800?"

That's the thing about tackling debt: Before you can sort out the tangled mess of financial problems, you have to stop adding to it. This isn't just a financial truth; it's a life truth. Something every newbie-dad gets when his infant son decides crayons are a snack.

It was back in the day, and as a "good dad," I went into panic mode the second I saw our youngest, Jake's mouth packed with crayons. I scrambled frantically to pick the rest up off the floor, thinking I could outpace his relentless gnawing by cleaning faster than he could chew. But for every crayon I grabbed, he managed to shove another into his mouth. It was drool (his), wax (the crayons'), and tears (mine) everywhere.

Krista spotted the insanity and shouted, "Stop it!"

Jake froze mid-chew and spit out the crayons. I stood there stiff as a saluting soldier. In that single second, the madness stopped. Only then was it time for the cleanup.

Debt works the same way. You can't start sorting it out until you stop making it worse. That's what you are about to do. And that's exactly what Dom did when he joined the Money Habit program. He stopped digging into deeper debt first, then he sorted out his circumstances.

When he pulled his credit reports,* Dom discovered his situation wasn't as dire as he'd feared. "I thought I was in tens of thousands of consumer debt and I'd never pay it off. But aside from a student loan, we owed only $8,000."

The Money Habit program gave Dom the confidence to face what he'd been avoiding: the truth about how much he owed.

In fact, he had built his debt up to be much worse than it was.

Our tendency to believe things are greatly different from the reality is called cognitive distortion. We humans amplify or minimize situations in our mind without considering what is true. Even if you've never heard of cognitive distortion, you've experienced it when someone jumps to conclusions before they hear you out, or when someone mistakes feelings for facts.

In Dom's case, he was caught in magnification, a kind of cognitive distortion that "makes a mountain out of a molehill." When we

---

* If you are a US resident, you can get one free credit report every year from each of the three major credit bureaus: Equifax, Experian, and TransUnion. Visit mymoneyhabit.com for more information on how to request your report.

magnify a situation, it can cause additional worry and stress, or we may disengage from the situation entirely, numb to reality. (Just like Dom's unopened envelopes and my "pile" of un-listened-to collection calls!) Either way, being caught in a cognitive distortion is a disadvantage because we don't know how to respond properly. The solution is always to get the facts and just the facts, ma'am. Then tackle it one step at a time, no matter how small the step.

Following the Money Habit system, Dom paid off the $8,000 within ten weeks. Ten weeks! He then started redirecting a portion of his monthly debt payments to that student loan. And the rest was redirected toward investments, the beginning of his "distant" dream.

And that 800 credit score club? You don't grow that kind of credit muscle in mere weeks, but it did improve to levels he hadn't seen in years. Not too shabby.

"Looking at my [Money Habit] accounts daily, that changed everything," he said. "I'm no longer scared about money. I look forward to handling it." Well done, Dom. Well done. Say goodbye to cognitive distortion.

You're already well on your way to getting a handle on your debt. You've removed the temptation of borrowing more, the biggest reason why people stay in the red. Next, you'll start paying down your old debt using one, or a combination, of the human-wired techniques I'm about to share with you. So if you've been avoiding dealing with your creditors, know that no matter how much you owe, you can knock it out. The first step is to stop digging.

Phase I: The Debt Freeze Method

Debt, like a mother-in-law, is not necessarily evil, just misunderstood and best handled in small doses. Over time, your relationship with debt (and maybe your mother-in-law) doesn't grow; it festers. Debt feeds on misuse, thrives on avoidance, and turns a stream of small mistakes into a deluge of drama. But there's good news. You can stop the storm before it starts.

In chapter 1, I shared the story of the relentless debt collection notices and phone calls I faced almost daily. I paid it all off, every penny, in five years and nine months. That's not an overnight fix, but big problems don't disappear overnight. What did happen on the very first day I took control was I felt power over debt, because I could stop the onslaught.

So, what happens on your day one? You'll do the same as Dom and I did. You'll stop the cycle.

We'll start with the debt freeze. In simple terms, this means reducing your expenses and modifying access to your credit, so you immediately halt the growth of your debt burden. This process forces you to tackle a very human tendency called "status quo bias." Once we establish a routine, even one that harms us, such as overspending, we tend to cling to it because it feels familiar. Breaking free means putting intentional barriers in the path of your bad money habits, forever disrupting the downward debt cycle.

You know the saying "If you're in a hole, stop digging"? That's the essence of the debt freeze. It doesn't fix or reduce your debt per se, but it fixes your debt habit. On day one, the debt freeze will align your mind and actions with a new identity: *I'm not a debtor anymore. Debt and me? We're never, ever, ever getting back together.*

The debt freeze is easy to implement; it has just three steps.

Step 1: Cut Unnecessary Expenses

The first step in the debt freeze is to cut back on anything you don't need to survive. And yes, this is a deliberate exception to what I said in chapter 4 about keeping a few joys. When debt is piling up, you need to stop the bleed. Fast. That debt is killing your future financial self. By slamming the brakes on spending, you free up cash to crush the debt. And when it comes to cutting, it's actually easier to strip everything out at once, then let a few joys seep back in, than to tiptoe through gradual cuts. Don't carve. Slash. Then rebuild.

Me? I broke the rule and carved slowly, like a ding-dong. First, I cut HBO. Didn't miss it. A couple of weeks later, I asked the fellas to skip our monthly guys' night out for dinner and drinks at the local bar and instead meet up at one of our homes. The irony? The conversations were better, there was no bar tab, and my buddy, nicknamed Silver-Back, casually said, "Glad we're doing this here, boys. I was starting to think I couldn't afford to hang out with you anymore."

My slow approach to cutting stuff went on for three months. At first, I realized I didn't miss the things I "needed." In fact, everything was replaceable with an alternative that was inevitably better. Then I realized dragging the process out triggered a repeating, painful conversation in my head that went like this: *Can I really do this? What will others think? Can I delay the decision?* Eventually, I had enough of my own self-imposed mother-in-law drama. Enough was enough. I had finally faced "the awful" and now was ready to rip off the Band-Aid, as Amber Dugger advises.

I remember selling my last bastion of ego, my Dodge Viper, and feeling an enormous sense of relief wash over me. I got cash for the car and used it to pay down a huge chunk of debt. I also was free of ongoing costs like car insurance and maintenance. But it wasn't just about ditching debt; I also shed the weight of an image I couldn't afford to keep. The massive relief was not just financial. It was emotional.

I dropped my forty-nine-dollars-a-month gym membership and started working out with my neighbor, Art Muti, which was way more fun and got way better results.

> ☑ **TAKE QUICK ACTION**
> You listed expenses in chapter 4. What things can you go without, even if it's just for a little while? What's redundant and begging to be consolidated? Which of these expenses do you vow to stop now? Because nobody is gonna stop you from financial independence. Got your list? Good. Do it. Now.

Step 2: Reduce Credit Card Limits

I then put in place a "commitment device," a technique designed to keep us on course with what we truly want, especially when we know we might resist. Using a commitment device is so human, you can even find it in ancient Greek mythology.

To prevent himself and his crew from following the sirens' call into dangerous rocky waters, Odysseus stuffed his crew's ears with beeswax and had his first mate tie him to a mast so he couldn't move. (We still use the metaphor of a siren call today to reference something that seems awesome on the surface but is actually super destructive. See? We've been doing stuff that isn't good for us for thousands of years!)

You can use commitment devices to prevent yourself from giving into a bad habit or to help you stick to a good habit. For example, to ensure I work out, I place my sneakers on the toilet seat, forcing me to grab them first thing in the morning when I go to the bathroom.

Credit cards are a great tool. They offer convenience, rewards, protection from fraud, and even insurance for rentals. But I'm only human, and I know what I fall victim to if I don't protect myself from myself: Parkinson's Law. If I have a credit card limit, I will find a way to justify spending to that limit. Since I have a natural tendency to abuse credit cards, I invoked a simple commitment device: I called my credit card company and asked them to lower my credit limit. On one card, I had a $5,000 limit, which I had them reduce to $2,000. It was an unusual request, but they honored it.

At the time, my debt was maxed out at $5,000, but the new limit forced me to pay it down to $2,000 before I could use the card again. This commitment device instilled discipline, helped me pay down debt without canceling the card, and set a lower ceiling to control future spending if I started to slip again.

When I asked the credit card company to lower my limit from $5,000 to $2,000 the agent said, "Sir, no one does that. More credit is better for your credit score when you manage the ratio." The thing was, I knew I couldn't manage, so all that nonsense didn't apply to me. And it doesn't apply to you either, so don't fall for it.

You could also hibernate a card without canceling it entirely. Some credit card companies allow you to temporarily deactivate your card for a set period. This serves as an effective temptation control while keeping the account open to preserve your credit history. To do this, call customer service and request a temporary deactivation. While your credit history won't be affected, the hibernation will cancel automatic payments linked to your card and prevent new purchases, and that could affect your credit score.

You may be wondering why I don't advocate canceling all your credit cards. The goal here is not to be cardless; in modern society, most of us depend on credit cards to go about our daily lives and there are key benefits beyond the "points."

We simply want to put up guardrails that work with our existing habits rather than try to become a person who never gets into trouble with their credit cards. If you don't, amazing. But most of us struggle with that, especially when life shows up with unexpected expenses, like medical emergencies. Hence the massive credit card debt Americans carry, which, at the time of this writing, is at $1.16 trillion.

> **☑ TAKE QUICK ACTION**
> Pick up the phone and call your credit card company (or companies) right now. Tell them to lower your credit limit or temporarily deactivate the card. Pick one or play varsity level and do both.

We good? Good! Step 2, done.

Step 3: Ask for Lower Credit Card Interest Rates

While you're asking your credit card companies to reduce your limit, request a reduction in your annual interest rate too. Say something like, "Thanks for adjusting my limit and setting up the temporary hold. I really value being a customer and want to continue using my card, but I'm considering switching to another company offering a lower introductory rate. If you can reduce my interest rate, I'd prefer to stay with you since I've been a loyal member for so long."

You may be met with resistance at first, but keep trying. Personally, I am batting around .800, meaning about 80 percent of the time they move me to a lower rate and 20 percent of the time they won't, so I cancel my account and go with a new no interest card or wait it out for a while with no new card at all.

And if you do cancel a card, remember you don't have to pay the full balance all at once. You can keep paying it off as you were before.

The debt freeze is about stopping the dig down. On day one, you're not just preventing new debt, you're paving the path forward. From that moment, debt becomes your past, not your future. And once you start, you'll realize that the hardest part wasn't doing it—it was deciding to begin.

> ☑ **TAKE QUICK ACTION**
>
> While you've got your credit card company on the line, ask for that lower interest rate. Don't overthink it; just say the words. If they say no, thank them, hang up, and call the next card company. You've got this. One call at a time, you're making debt your history, not your future.

I'm assuming you got this done. Congrats! That's step 3 checked off the list. Go ahead and have a sip of that gross bourbon tea of yours. Or better yet, celebrate with your own, no cost, version of a victory lap!

Phase II: The Debt Snowball Method

The best way to eat an elephant? No, it's not one bite at a time. The best way is to *not eat it at all*. Instead, grab a burger or a veggie patty, if that's your thing. You need to feel good, enjoy the process, and get those good internal juices flowing. If it feels miserable or unnatural, you'll quit before you're done. Starting small, with something satisfying, is the key to tackling anything massive. And, really, who the hell eats elephants anyway?

You may have heard of the debt snowball. Dave Ramsey, author of *The Total Money Makeover*, popularized this term, but the concept goes back to 1938. Harvard psychologist B. F. Skinner documented reinforcement theory, identifying how small, early wins condition us to repeat them. In a nutshell, Skinner's theory applied to finance serves us by wiping out small debts fast to get those wins under our belt.

As Ramsey recommended in his book, rather than try to pay off the debt with the highest interest rate first, pay off the smallest debt first, regardless of interest rate. The idea is you will get a dopamine rush and a big dose of pride when you pay off a debt, any debt, once and for all. That, in turn, will help you sustain momentum until all your debt is paid off. This approach does not make logical sense, because higher interest rates cost more, but it surely works with how you are made.

When I read Ramsey's explanation for the debt snowball, I got it right away. You see, I wanted to pay back a $3,500 loan my longtime friend Chris gave me when I badly needed the money. I kept trying to pay down that loan and dodge bill collectors, and became more and more frustrated with my lack of progress.

After nearly three years of failing to make headway, I felt defeated. It seemed like I wasn't making any progress by chipping away at everything. So I tried the debt snowball method of just getting the first debt off my plate forever. I had a store credit card with a low limit, maxed out at a balance of $500.

I kept paying minimum amounts on other bills and periodic bits and pieces to Chris's loan (I agreed to pay him "whenever" I could), but I cranked up the installments on my store card by concentrating any spare cash I could find, here. That meant I stopped my attempts to pay above my minimum payments on my other cards. And I adjusted down my WANTS allocations. Combining these two moves, I freed up enough cash to move from the minimum payment of $25 a month to around $150 a month for the store debt. Within three months, the debt was paid in full. Done! It felt so good tearing up that statement and then burning it (true story). The best part was calling the store and canceling the card. Then I cut it into as many small pieces as I could and tossed it into the recycle bin. (Don't burn plastic! It's toxic!)

The debt snowball worked with the very first card. It seemed manageable and felt satisfying. I had downed my first (non-elephant) "burger," and I was hooked. With the minimum installments I had been making to pay off the store card ($25/month) now freed up, I added them to the payments I was already making on the next debt with the smallest balance, an outstanding $1,500 medical bill. I again looked for extra cash I could spare to target this next debt. I quickly paid it off. And then did the same with the next. All the while, I kept paying minimums on everything else, shared my strategy with Chris (who supported it), and gave him updates to stay accountable.

Over time, I realized the debt snowball technique is a really good place to start, because of the behavioral necessity to feel a sense of accomplishment, particularly after a long time feeling bad about yourself. But staying with the same method exclusively is not fiscally smart.

I had a credit card with a $12,000 balance. I had convinced the credit card company to lower the rate from 25 percent to 22 percent, but even with that (minor) reduction, I would still pay a huge amount in interest because it would take a year or more before that credit card was up in my debt snowball lineup. The key is to align emotion (what feels good) with logic (what is good).

THE DEBT SNOWBALL METHOD

Debt Name	Balance	Interest Rate	Minimum Payment
Store credit card	$500	10%	$25
Medical bill	$1,500	0%	$50
Personal loan	$3,500	0%	$0
Furniture loan	$8,000	15%	$100
Credit card	$12,000	22%	$450
Student loan	$35,000	5%	$300

The debt snowball method (example). Rooted in B. F. Skinner's reinforcement theory and popularized by Dave Ramsey, this method tackles debt from smallest to largest balance. List all your debts, the interest rates, and minimum payments to get a clear picture of what can be tackled first. Sort your list from smallest to largest balance. Extra dollars go toward the smallest debt first, in this case, the $500 store credit card, while minimum payments continue on the rest. The goal: Score quick wins and build momentum.

We start with the snowball process to build confidence and establish behavioral momentum. However, true financial optimization doesn't happen when you're chipping away at a 0 percent loan while a 22 percent debt lingers. The objective is to get a few quick wins under your belt, then flip the script into something far more powerful.

☑ TAKE QUICK ACTION

Identify your smallest debt right now. Don't overthink it. Pull up your balances and pick the smallest one. That's our target. Commit every extra dollar you can to paying it off quickly. The quick win of wiping out even a tiny debt will build good habits and create momentum. Once that small debt is gone, celebrate (no pricey splurges!) and move on to the next smallest debt. You're on a habit-building winning streak now!

Phase III: The Debt Avalanche Method

The debt snowball gives you behavioral momentum; the debt avalanche gives you financial momentum. This method tackles the costliest high-interest debt, which makes the most financial sense. By now, you've experienced the satisfaction of clearing debts, so you're ready to optimize your efforts.

When considering how to pay down debt, you should consider three logical factors:

1 The amount of the debt
2 The interest rate
3 The consequence

What do I mean by consequence? Missing a credit card payment can lead to penalties or collections, adding to your debt. Failing to repay a personal loan, like the one I owed Chris, could damage a valuable relationship and my self-respect. While the amount and interest rate matter, the consequence often carries the most weight.

Now, with all three forces aligned—amount, interest rate, and consequence—plus the behavioral momentum from early wins, the debt avalanche becomes the final tool we need in debt destruction.

Step 1: Build on Wins from the Debt Snowball
Continue paying minimums on all debts while now redirecting the focus to the highest-interest debt or the one with the most severe consequences. Direct as much as possible toward this priority debt.

Step 2: Pay One Priority Debt and Then Another
Once the highest-interest or highest-consequence debt is gone, shift to the next. By this stage, you're tackling debts in order of financial impact, ensuring the least amount of money is lost to interest. Continue redirecting freed-up funds to accelerate payments on remaining debts.

Moving from the debt snowball (early wins) to now the debt avalanche (big wins), you optimize your money habits. This method balances the emotional payoff of early wins with the long-term financial benefits of reducing high-cost debt. The avalanche I got going meant splitting freed-up funds between high-interest credit cards and repaying Chris more aggressively. Small debts (and big debts) that were low interest were still being addressed with minimum payments. But my focus was now on crushing the costly (high interest and high consequence) stuff. Along with the falling debt came the best part: falling stress.

As I worked the debt avalanche method, I stayed in close communication with Chris about my strategy. That last part was the smartest thing I did, because it maintained trust. I remember the day I sent Chris the final payment on the loan. I said, "Hey, Chris, we agreed to interest. I owe you another five hundred dollars."

"Are you kidding?" he said. "You owe nothing more. Thanks for being true to your word."

True to your word. That was the greatest moment of my debt-free journey.

THE DEBT AVALANCHE METHOD

Debt Name	Balance	Interest Rate	Minimum Payment
~~Store credit card~~	~~$500~~	~~10%~~	~~$25~~
~~Medical bill~~	~~$1,500~~	~~0%~~	~~$50~~
Credit card	$12,000	22%	$450
Furniture loan	$8,000	15%	$100
Personal loan	$3,500	0% (high consequence)	$0 (communication)
Student loan	$35,000	5%	$300

The debt avalanche method. Once you have a few small wins under your belt, shift to tackling debts that have the highest consequences for nonpayment. Each crossed-out debt builds confidence. And by eliminating the most damaging debts first, you reduce your total debt load and emotional weight faster and more efficiently. That's why the personal loan, while interest-free, comes before the student loan. Because, for me, risking a friendship costs more than 5 percent interest ever will.

With the debt avalanche, the focus shifts from the smallest debts to those with the highest interest rates while factoring in personal consequences. The store credit card and medical bill, already paid off using the debt snowball method, remain listed but are crossed off because they are done with (nice!). Now, the focus moves to the credit card, which carries a 22 percent interest rate, making it the most financially draining.

All freed-up funds from previous wins are directed toward the credit card while maintaining minimum payments on the remaining debts. The "minimum payment" for the personal loan, however, is active communication. A promise kept, and a relationship maintained. Once the credit card is paid off, the next priority is the furniture loan at 15 percent, given its high interest.

After that comes paying down the personal loan. While it has a 0 percent interest rate, it carries significant personal consequences if left unpaid. Active communication buys some time, but it doesn't eliminate the obligation. Delaying too long risks lost trust and possibly a lost friend. For this reason, the personal loan takes precedence over the student loan, which has both a higher interest rate (5 percent) and balance, but a lower personal impact.

By tackling debts in this interest/consequence sequence, the debt avalanche has you now financially optimized. That is the ultimate money habit.

> ☑ **TAKE QUICK ACTION**
> Identify your highest-interest debt now and shift your focus to crushing it. Keep making minimum payments on all others but throw every extra dollar at that costly balance. Start your avalanche and feel the financial weight lift as the high-interest debts fall!

The Power of Negotiation

Humans are made for negotiation and compromise. That's how we thrive. Start with an intention and then go for the ask. Approach it with integrity and compassion, for both the person you owe and for yourself. Debt isn't set in stone; it's written in sand.

When I pressed Dom Anderson to tell me how he paid down $8,000 in debt in ten weeks, I was surprised to learn he didn't pay that amount in full. A big chunk of that debt was $5,000 he and his wife, Princess, owed on their car. They had purchased it with a subprime lender, which meant they were paying outrageous interest on the car. They'd probably already paid for the value of the car a couple of times over.

With the newfound confidence the Money Habit system gave him, and a quick check of his FIX account, he was able to negotiate a lower payoff for the car loan and the amount will surprise you. It sure surprised me!

"I called the finance company," Dom explained, "and I said, 'Look, we're paying this car off. We have the money. There's no point in continuing to make payments when we can just knock it off, but I'm not paying five thousand. What can we do here?'"

The agent offered Dom a payoff of $4,700, a $300 reduction, but he wasn't having it.

"I said, 'That's too much. I want to speak to someone else.' So she passed me off to another department."

The next agent offered Dom a payoff of $1,500. A huge difference! But Dom still wasn't having it.

"I told them, 'Nope, I still don't like that. We did subprime lending because my credit was horrible. I have already paid you the worth of this car three times over. You have already made a killing off me, so why do you feel you need to kill me off? Let's get this knocked out.'"

The agent offered him another payoff amount: $950! Dom took the deal.

The finance company had initially offered him $4,700 and he negotiated it down to $950. Well done!

Next, Dom tackled his past due AT&T bill. He and Princess had switched phone service companies mid-billing cycle, and AT&T claimed they still owed $300. Dom learned this only after pulling his credit report; the amount was in collections.

He called the collections company and offered them a deal. He would pay $150, half of the bill, and that was it.

"The collection agent said he had to talk to his manager, and then he came back and said they couldn't do it, that we'd have to pay the debt in full," Dom explained. "I told him, 'Have a good one. It was nice talking to you.'"

The agent tried to keep Dom on the phone and said they would take his $150 as a monthly payment toward the $300 debt.

"I said, 'I told you this was my offer. I know you bought my debt from the company for less than what I owe. Either I'll never pay this bill or you can take what I'm offering you now. Up to you.'"

Dang, that's intense. When Dom told me this story, I wanted to go back in time and see the look on the debt collector's face. The best part is, Dom didn't give up. You see, he did want to pay the debt. He wasn't trying to get out of it. He just didn't want to pay all the inflated fees associated with it. And he leveraged his knowledge of how collection agencies work to get the deals he wanted. Integrity happens when you know the truth of both your position and the collector's.

"The next day, I just called the collection agency back and tried again. I got a different person who was willing to make the deal, and we got it done."

Dom called every single collection agency, some multiple times on different days, and negotiated deals. With every call, he was polite, told them he wanted to pay the debt, and asserted that he would not pay the full amount. This is where integrity and tenacity are the ultimate debt destroying one-two punch.

You don't have to play the collection agency's or lenders' games. You can negotiate big reductions that will help you pay off your debt faster. You just need to be poised, polite, and persistent. And looking at your FIX account will give you the poise/confidence you need to make these calls as it tells you how much you are willing to lay out to pay off that debt.

If you need inspiration to tackle negotiation, take it from Dom, who told me, "Who can stop me from doing this but myself?"

> ☑ **TAKE QUICK ACTION**
>
> Check your FIX account to know how much you can offer. Call a creditor or collection agency and say, "I want to pay this off, but I can't pay the full amount. What can we work out?" Stay polite, be persistent, and don't settle on the first call if it doesn't work. Once you strike a deal, confirm it in writing, pay, and celebrate. That's it. Simple, direct, done!

Don't Sacrifice Your WANTS and DREAMS

We have been taught to focus on needs before wants, on paying down debt before funding our dreams. It's the same in business. We are taught that profit is whatever we have left over after we pay all our expenses first. They say you make money only after everything else has been addressed. They say you need to be debt-free before you will have money for your vision. They are wrong.

I mean logically, it makes sense you will have money left over only from what you haven't spent. But behaviorally they are wrong.

If we don't address the savings first, we never get around to it. Flipping that formula is the cornerstone of the Profit First system that has helped save more than one million businesses worldwide. Simply by taking their profit *before* they pay any expenses, even if it's only a tiny percentage, business owners ensure they will always be profitable. And man, that PROFIT account sitting there at their bank changes something in them. Even if it only has five bucks in it, that account makes them feel differently about the blood, sweat, and tears they are putting into running their business.

The same principle works for anyone who earns an income. Think of your WANTS and DREAMS accounts like a business owner's PROFIT account. You must pay yourself first; meaning, you must give yourself some of that financial joy first. Paying necessary bills doesn't make us feel good, necessarily. Waiting to do something fun only once everything else is done makes us feel deprived. We are more likely to spend money on things that make us happy now because when we do, we get a dopamine hit.

This is a classic example of temporal discounting, a behavioral tendency first studied extensively by psychologists George Ainslie and Richard Herrnstein. The human inclination is to value immediate rewards and desires over future needs, wants, or even dreams. Our brains are wired to prioritize the instant dopamine hit of spending now, while the abstract idea of a rent payment two weeks away holds little emotional weight.

By transferring a small percentage of your income to your WANTS and DREAMS accounts, you harness your natural desire for instant gratification and use it strategically. This simple act satisfies your brain's craving for a dopamine hit, the chemical rush we feel when we indulge in something enjoyable, like buying new clothes or going out to dinner. More importantly, seeing that money set aside creates a powerful shift. It transforms your desires into tangible goals, making them feel real and attainable. Your mind begins to visualize the reward, reinforcing your motivation and satisfaction. In essence, you're turning the dopamine hit into a tool that works for your financial success, rather than against it.

I've found that when people who participate in the Money Habit system have a lot of debt, they believe they can't use their after-expense money on anything except paying down that debt. So they sacrifice. They say no to a night out with their BFF. They eat PB&J for lunch every day. (Been there.) They cut all their luxuries and niceties and devote every last penny to paying down credit card principal, interest, and fees. But then the humanness kicks in.

Eventually, that deprivation gets to us, and we cave. We buy something on that same credit card, or we blow part of our paycheck, just to get that dopamine fix, man. From a psychological perspective, it is the pattern of scarcity and overcompensation. We deprive ourselves until, damn it, we "can't take it anymore" and then the collapse of a spending binge or other financial indiscretions happen. All of this is preventable, not through more discipline, but through more reward.

We need to experience wins while gaining control of our finances, and those wins come from accumulating money in our WANTS and DREAMS accounts. We are made to accumulate; it's in our DNA. This tendency is rooted in our evolutionary past and explained by optimal foraging theory (OFT). In the past, survival meant gathering resources efficiently. Today, instead of physical stuff, the Money Habit system helps us accumulate cash on a simple, efficient basis.

OFT shows that humans naturally focus on actions that provide the greatest benefit with the least effort. Early humans didn't just gather berries for one meal; they stockpiled enough to last for days. It wasn't "Ugh, me get woolly mammoth steak for dinner tonight," but "Ugh, I go on big hunt to feed family for long time." Then, when they caught the woolly mammoth, they carved it up and would feed their families for weeks. That instinct to maximize results from their effort and stretch resources over time ensured survival.

The same principle applies to modern humans. Particularly around money. Income comes in bursts: a handful of berries (e.g., paychecks) or big mammoths (e.g., bonuses). While prehistoric humans were reminded constantly of their hunger, prompting them to ration, our modern life doesn't come with those relentless pangs.

Instead, we experience rolling financial waves. Payday brings a false sense of abundance, making us feel flush with cash and eager to spend. Spending often too much, too fast, on too many things. But as the weeks pass, the money runs thin, and suddenly, payday can't come fast enough. Then the cycle repeats: overspending, followed by overstretching, again and again.

The Money Habit system channels this instinct by allocating money into WANTS and DREAMS accounts, making it easy to see what can be enjoyed now (a few berries) and what should be saved for later (the rest of the berries).

As these accounts grow, we get dopamine hits. Not just from spending, but from anticipating future rewards. Seeing progress feels like a win; dopamine is released, reinforcing the saving habit. And when we've saved enough to make a guilt-free purchase, we get another dopamine rush from rewarding ourselves.

The beauty of this system? These aren't reckless splurges. They're planned, joyful indulgences that keep us on track with bills and obligations. And let's face it, dopamine, the brain's natural joyful juice, is the most powerful drug out there. When we use it to our advantage, it doesn't just flow; it fuels our financial success.

Every year, my family goes on a trip. One year, it was a nice vacation rental and a trip to Mount Vernon to see George Washington's home. Another year, it was cave exploring. As I write this, we are planning the biggest of big Michalowicz family trips—we are heading to Ireland! That's a lot of Michalowiczes on an island of lots of Mc-somethings.

Time with our family is my greatest joy, and so with each disbursement to our DREAMS account, I get a little buzz knowing that trip is rapidly approaching and will be guilt-free. My wife and I have no worries about the money we spend on the trip. We will be fully present and enjoy ourselves, without any concern for how we will cover the trip, because it's already covered. Kind of like going on an all-inclusive cruise, where everything is paid for in advance.

Let Self-Punishment Go

Talking to Dom, I remembered my own insecurity about facing debt collectors. The way I stalked my mail carrier daily to make sure my wife and neighbors didn't see the envelopes with red lettering in big, bold fonts that read: "Account Delinquent," "Collection Notice," and my favorite, as in bury-my-face-in-shame least favorite, "Legal Notice." I kept my monument of unopen bills stashed out of sight while I tried to come up with a way to win the lottery or the equivalent. And I tried to cloak the shame I felt because I had gotten my family into so much debt.

"When you're scared about money and avoiding it, it can cause a lot of problems in your marriage," I said to Dom.

Dom nodded. "I used to be a horrible piece of crap. I started changing my ways and gaining my wife's trust with the finances and all that other good stuff, and that changed everything for us."

Of course Dom wasn't a "horrible piece of crap," no more than I was, but it sure can feel that way when you struggle with debt over and over and, one more unopened bill, over again. You aren't horrible either. You're human. Yes, you may have regrets, and that's okay. But punishing yourself for your regrets is something else. You may think, *Easy for you to say, Mike. You don't know my mistakes.* Fair enough. But here I'll tell you one of my biggest mistakes, a real doofus move that I deeply regret.

I took out a $100,000 small business administration loan to help me grow my business, then started siphoning some of that money to cover some of my living expenses. I put the rest of the expenses on a credit card, so I was draining the loan while watching my credit card balances climb higher and higher. You may think that was the doofus move, but really it was when I had $10,000 left of the loan and rather than invest it into my business, I played financial roulette and invested it in the stock market. I had this desperate idea that the best use of that last $10,000 was to gamble it on penny stocks. Of course the stock I invested in tanked. Of course!

Self-punishment is debilitating. It keeps you from taking action. As the bills pile up and the debt skyrockets, self-punishment keeps you down, digging your hole deeper and deeper. I had every reason to punish myself for that doofus decision, but I didn't. I paid back the loan and made it right. Though I will always regret that move, I won't rake myself over the coals for it, because that would keep me tied up in the cycle of shame.

If you're in debt, that's not a sign that you're a bad person. It's not even a sign that you made bad decisions; some credit card debt is just unavoidable. Stop berating yourself, so you can start climbing out of the hole, bit by bit. If Dom and I can do it, you can too. I'm sure of it.

A final thought on debt and its emotional weight: the term "mortgage" originates from the Latin words "mors" (death) and "gage" (pledge). A mortgage is, quite literally, a "death pledge." Ain't that sumpin'.

GET 'ER DONE SUMMARY
STOP DIGGING. START CLIMBING.

1. **Get the facts.** You can't fix what you won't face. Visit mymoneyhabit.com for tools to pull your credit report and repair any damage. Write down exactly what you owe, to whom, and at what interest rates. No guessing.

2. **Implement the debt freeze today.** Cut one unnecessary expense *today*. Then call your credit card companies and 1) lower your credit limit, 2) ask for a reduced interest rate, and 3) request a temporary deactivation. Do one, two, or all three. It's time to step off the debt treadmill.

3. **Choose your first debt snowball target.** Target your smallest balance and hit it with every extra dollar. Don't worry about the interest rate yet—this is about momentum, not math. Crush that first debt, feel the win, and roll that payment into the next one.

4. **Trigger your debt avalanche.** After a few wins, aim higher. Target your debt with the highest interest *or* biggest consequences. Keep minimum payments on the rest. Funnel every extra penny to this monster until it's gone. Then repeat. Logic now takes over where momentum started.

7

Build a Better Financial Future Now

YOU MAY THINK this chapter is about investing your money. You're not wrong. I do want you to start investing some of your income to help it grow. But there is a single investment that yields the most monetarily, has the fastest returns, and you will likely enjoy. And yet this investment vehicle doesn't require a financial manager, a financial platform, a financial anything.

If you haven't figured it out by now, the number one investment vehicle of all time is investing in yourself. By expanding your mind and abilities, you expand your wallet. I want you to invest in your *future self*, and I want you to start today.

And this is exactly why your FUTURE account is so critical. This account isn't just a placeholder for your future retirement; it is also a fund dedicated to actively building your future self. It's there to help you acquire new skills, enroll in that course, attend that seminar, or make that career move without hesitation. To build an even better future, build an even better future you.

In his book *Be Your Future Self Now*, Benjamin P. Hardy wrote: "As a species, we haven't evolved to plan twenty years into the future. As a rule, our decision-making is myopic, shortsighted, and lacks imagination. We're heavily incentivized to seek rewards in the present, which can greatly cost our long-term Future Selves."

Hardy says we're wired to be "distracted by the short term," rather than make decisions for the long term. So this is why, when we're just trying to get by, it's nearly impossible to think about what we need to do today to have a better day tomorrow, let alone a better day two decades down the road. And these decisions we make to get by can be darn expensive. As Hardy says, "[Prioritizing short-term wants will] cost your Future Self greatly, putting them deeper in debt in all ways." *In all ways*, not just literal financial debt. Your mental and physical health, your relationships and connections, your earning ability, your spiritual well-being.

The fantastic news? As you know well by now, The Money Habit works *with* your natural tendencies; it doesn't require you to become someone else. That means while you (as in all of us humans) are wired for the short-term rewards, the system ensures that you don't have to try to focus on the long term. At least not when it comes to financial investments. You can, as the saying goes, "set it and forget it." You'll be investing in your future without thinking much about it. In fact, you probably won't notice it all.

Don't Think About It

The best financial investment is the one you put in place and give space.

Some people have a compulsion to look at their investment accounts and tweak them, hoping to "buy low and sell high," predicting stock market trends. In real estate, it is the flippers' mentality. In crypto, it's the "buy by dawn and sell by dusk" mindset. When we try these approaches, we turn investing into a lottery game. Our investments will most likely underperform or, worst-case scenario, we'll lose them all.

A study documented by Berkley.edu revealed that 99 percent of day traders consistently underperformed the long-term "set it and forget it" investors. Not to mention the emotional swings of the "dawn to dusk" investors. The same article points out that traders rarely acknowledge that luck is the main factor when they do get a "hit," and instead attribute it to skill and gamble more.

Everyday investors can also get too involved in trying to "play the game." They see the stock market plummeting on the news and race to get out before "things get worse." But their haste is what makes things worse for them.

Let me give you the shortest, most effective lesson in investing. If you're not a professional investor who has dedicated your entire life to mastering the markets, real estate, or crypto, here's all you need to know distilled from decades of experience and advice from the greats. Do two things:*

1 Invest in stock index funds. These are mutual funds designed to mirror the performance of a market index like the Nasdaq or S&P 500.

2 Employ the dollar-cost average system. This means investing a fixed amount of money at regular intervals, no matter what the market is doing.

That's it. Two things. History proves you will outpace every speculative investor and the majority of the pros to boot. Warren Buffett, arguably the greatest investor in history, said that for nearly everyone, these two things, index funds and dollar-cost averaging, are the best tactics for success.

I majored in finance in college, worked with dozens of hedge fund clients, and studied the strategies of countless experts. And after all that, one guy and his one minute of advice could have saved me years of distractions, confusion, and misunderstanding—the unnecessary complexity I thought investing required. And the losses, of course. The countless missed financial gains, because I stepped out when I should have stayed in.

---

* I'm not your financial advisor, and this isn't investment advice in the legal sense. But I'd tell my best friend the same thing: Skip the hype, skip the guesswork, and stick to what works. Unless you've got an expert you fully trust (or are one), index funds win. It might not seem sexy, but sticking with the boring stuff that works? Kinda sexy.

According to Investopedia, "Many investors fail to remain invested in stocks when a rebound occurs. In fact, they tend to jump back in only when most of the gains have already been achieved." The buy high, sell low practice, the website notes, tends to crush investor returns.

We let our emotions, our fears, and our regrets rule our decision-making. (There's that short-term wiring again.) Stick with your investments (ideally, forget about them) and never let panic or emotion drive your decisions. Why does this strategy work? Because the most powerful force in the financial world is compounding.

If you put a percentage of your income into historically good investments, regardless of the momentary ups and downs, over time, they grow. All you need to do is set up an automatic allocation for investments. Don't touch them and let your money go to work for you.

An easy way to do this is through your company's 401(k) program (or similar), which automatically deducts a percentage of your paycheck—another account you don't have to think about, just like your Money Habit bank accounts. The account is just there, and it does its job. Your employer may even offer a contribution matching benefit, where they put in an additional portion on top of yours. That's free money!

But can putting away a small portion of your paycheck really make that much of a difference?

From Pennies to Millions

Let's imagine you place a bet on a round of golf. For the first hole, the wager is one penny. At the second hole, the bet doubles to two cents. The third hole doubles again to four cents, and so on, for all eighteen holes.

At first, the penny bets seem trivial. One cent, two cents, four cents. For the part of life we're living right now, the hole we're "playing," it seems like nothing. Even by the tenth hole, the bet is only $5.12.

But by the eighteenth hole, that small, seemingly insignificant penny has grown to $1,310.72. Yes, you read that right. One penny grew to $1,310.72 in a single round of golf, just by doubling the bet at each hole. This is the power of compounding. What seems tiny at the beginning, barely noticeable, becomes massive over time. And the earlier you start, the more impactful it becomes.

The key is to play the long game and trust the process, even when the growth is invisible, and even when you, like all us mortals, get caught up in emotional, short-term thinking. Playing the long game is easy when you follow the Money Habit system because your investments are out of sight and therefore, out of mind.

A penny may seem disposable, valueless. And on its own it is. But a penny paired with time is profoundly valuable. So, what is your "penny"? What amount is small enough that you won't feel it in your day-to-day life? Can you store away one penny per day? What about a dime or a dollar? For most folks, one dollar per day is "disposable." So let's apply that no-brainer amount to compound interest.

The average rate of return over time in the stock market, adjusted for inflation and using the S&P index, is 7 percent. Bonds yield about 2.5 percent (adjusted for inflation). Stocks are considered riskier than bonds. If your investments included an equal mix of stocks and bonds,* you would have a return of 4.75 percent after inflation.

After one year of saving one dollar a day with a 4.75 percent annual interest rate compounded daily, the balance would be approximately $373.83. After two years of saving one dollar a day with a 4.75 percent annual interest rate compounded daily, the balance would be approximately $765.85. Seven-hundred-something bucks may seem like squat. I suspect, with your current lifestyle, you could find a way to use up that money within seconds.

---

* Speak with your financial advisor to get a professional recommendation on your investments. If you have a 401(k) you surely have access to the advisor for the plan. Ask your human resources representative or boss for the introduction.

As the years go by, that's when things get interesting. If you don't access your one-dollar-a-day account and keep the daily contributions going, here are your balances by the end of years three, four, and five:

Year 3: $1,176.93
Year 4: $1,608.01
Year 5: $2,060.06

What if you simply saved one dollar a day in a "cash stash" spot in your house for five years? You'd have $1,825. In an investment account, the 4.75 percent compound interest gives you an additional $235.06 that you wouldn't have earned stuffing George Washingtons into a cookie jar.

Maybe an extra two hundred bucks and change is not worth it to you. Remember, we're playing the long game here. So let's look at ten years into the future. That may seem far away, but if you reflect on your life, doesn't ten years ago seem like it just happened? (Maybe that's just me.)

After ten years investing one dollar a day, you'd have $4,672.34. If you stuffed the money under your mattress, you'd have $3,650. That's more than $1,000 in money you didn't have to clock in to earn. Now we're getting somewhere.

Let's leap ahead in ten- and twenty-year increments.

$1/WEEK INVESTMENT

Number of Years	Investment Balance	Cash Stash Balance
5	$2,060.06	$1,825.00
20	$12,185.28	$7,300.00
30	$24,265.84	$10,950.00
50	$74,925.82	$18,250.00

Do you see it? In thirty years, investing one dollar a day with a 4.75 percent annual interest rate compounded daily more than doubles your contribution. And in fifty years, it *quadruples* the amount you invested. And these examples are based on investing just *one dollar a day,* one hundred pennies.

Imagine what you could do with twenty dollars a week? That's $2.86 a day. For that you get the following:

$20/WEEK INVESTMENT

Number of Years	Investment Balance	Cash Stash Balance
5	$5,891.01	$5,219.00
20	$34,845.38	$20,878.00
30	$69,391.27	$31,317.00
50	$214,259.97	$52,195.00

Another example. If you invest $100 a week:

$100/WEEK INVESTMENT

Number of Years	Investment Balance	Cash Stash Balance
5	$29,425.63	$26,000.00
20	$174,052.84	$104,000.00
30	$346,609.75	$156,000.00
50	$1,070,229.62	$260,000.00

And the last example, $500 a week:

$500/WEEK INVESTMENT

Number of Years	Investment Balance	Cash Stash Balance
5	$147,128.15	$130,000.00
20	$870,264.20	$520,000.00
30	$1,733,048.74	$780,000.00
50	$5,351,148.10	$1,300,000.00

Pretty amazing. The key is to start investing your pennies and dollars now. Truly, right now. Don't wait until tomorrow. Don't wait to finish the book, let alone this paragraph. Don't say you are too old. And oh please don't say you are too young.

> ☑ **TAKE QUICK ACTION**
>
> Put money into an interest-yielding account starting today. Make it routine. Make it automatic. I do it daily. You can do it daily, or weekly, or when your paycheck hits.

As I shared with the *Frequency × Amount = Time to Goal* formula in chapter 1, I've found that if you contribute smaller amounts more often, you don't feel or see big drops in your accounts. Putting a dollar away each day is thirty dollars once a month. These small, consistent actions quietly build into a substantial compounded fortune.

What Is Your Investment Goal?

If you aren't sure how many dollars you will need to save to live the life you want in the future, I've created a chart to help you figure it out. First, find your goal on the chart. Don't worry, I will help you if you don't know what your goal should be. Do you want $100,000 in reserves, $500,000, $1 million, or even $10 million? Then, set your timeline. Do you want to reach that goal in five years, ten years, twenty-five years, or fifty years? Looking at the chart, you'll discover how much you'd have to allocate for investments each day or week to reach that goal.

Before you say, "But I don't know how much I want/need to save. I don't know when I want/need it by." I get it. And don't worry if you don't know. I surely didn't. But I found a way and will show you.

Know this: The feeling of not knowing has a name. It's called being human. Feeling unsure or uncomfortable is completely normal, so embrace it. It's okay not to have all the answers right now. I'll guide you through a strategy to determine how much to set aside for investments.

First, let's look at some charts that show you the investment you need to make to achieve a goal in savings.

$100,000 SAVINGS GOAL (FUNDING FREQUENCY)

	Daily	Weekly	Monthly
Within 5 years	$48.65	$341.51	$1,479.86
Within 10 years	$21.46	$150.61	$652.64
Within 25 years	$5.73	$40.22	$174.28
Within 50 years	$1.34	$9.42	$40.80

$250,000 SAVINGS GOAL (FUNDING FREQUENCY)

	Daily	Weekly	Monthly
Within 5 years	$121.63	$853.76	$3,699.64
Within 10 years	$53.64	$376.53	$1,631.61
Within 25 years	$14.32	$100.55	$435.71
Within 50 years	$3.35	$23.54	$102.01

$500,000 SAVINGS GOAL (FUNDING FREQUENCY)

	Daily	Weekly	Monthly
Within 5 years	$234.26	$1,707.53	$7,399.29
Within 10 years	$107.28	$753.05	$3,263.22
Within 25 years	$28.65	$201.10	$871.42
Within 50 years	$6.71	$47.08	$204.02

$1 MILLION SAVINGS GOAL (FUNDING FREQUENCY)

	Daily	Weekly	Monthly
Within 5 years	$486.53	$3,415.06	$14,798.58
Within 10 years	$214.57	$1,506.10	$6,526.44
Within 25 years	$57.30	$402.19	$1,742.84
Within 50 years	$13.42	$94.16	$408.04

$5 MILLION SAVINGS GOAL (FUNDING FREQUENCY)

	Daily	Weekly	Monthly
Within 5 years	$2,432.64	$17,075.28	$73,992.89
Within 10 years	$1,072.84	$7,530.51	$32,632.21
Within 25 years	$286.49	$2,010.97	$8,714.20
Within 50 years	$67.08	$470.82	$2,040.22

$10 MILLION SAVINGS GOAL (FUNDING FREQUENCY)

	Daily	Weekly	Monthly
Within 5 years	$4,865.29	$34,150.57	$147,985.79
Within 10 years	$2,145.68	$15,061.02	$65,264.41
Within 25 years	$572.99	$4,021.94	$17,428.40
Within 50 years	$134.15	$941.64	$4,080.45

$25 MILLION SAVINGS GOAL (FUNDING FREQUENCY)

	Daily	Weekly	Monthly
Within 5 years	$12,163.22	$85,376.42	$369,964.47
Within 10 years	$5,364.20	$37,652.54	$163,161.03
Within 25 years	$1,432.47	$10,054.85	$43,571.01
Within 50 years	$335.38	$2,354.11	$10,201.12

Savings goal. These tables show you the level of investments needed to reach various targets over different spans.

The numbers above apply regardless of the financial season you're in. These are fixed dollar amounts (not percentages) that you'll need to save in an interest-yielding account with an average return of 4.75 percent over time. While the season doesn't directly impact the required amounts, your approach may differ. For instance, in the Activate season, your focus is on utilizing money, so your investing goals might be minimal. In contrast, during the Fund season, you might aim for more ambitious investment targets.

Other factors, such as your age and future lifestyle aspirations, also play a role. For example, if you're forty years old and in the Fund season, and you want to enjoy a more lavish lifestyle by the time you're fifty, you'll need to set a ten-year investment goal accordingly.

If you'd like to really dig into the numbers and nail down the investment goal that will work best for you, I have a free calculator and something even better at mymoneyhabit.com. The something better is an AI prompt/script. You can simply plug in any numbers you think of, just like if you and I were doing this together over a couple of beers and a plate of nachos.

And although the charts above show you million-dollar goals, you don't have to choose those numbers. Maybe you want to figure out how to invest enough to buy an RV in twenty years. You can use the calculator to figure that out too. The American Dream is *not* synonymous with being a millionaire. That's just a number. You get to decide what your American Dream looks like, and how much you need to live it. But I think I know what it basically is for you (and all of us): time to do what you want, how you want, when you want. And the right amount of savings will get you more than the RV; it can set you up to have money coming to you automatically because your savings are earning your living for you. That is the financial freedom I am talking about.

But what if you already have savings? Here's how it works: Say your goal is $500,000, and you've already got $250,000 saved (well done, by the way). Just subtract what you already have from your goal: $500,000 – $250,000 = $250,000. That $250,000 becomes your target, and that's the number you select in the chart. Simple. It's not about starting from scratch; it's about knowing your gap and closing it.

Two Rules to Plan By

I won't tease it anymore; here's how to find your investment goal: If you want to fund your financial freedom, you'll need to think about how much you'll need to live on after you stop getting a paycheck. The best rule of thumb is to live on "interest only," meaning you don't have to chew down your principal, the balance in your investment accounts, because that's when the clock starts on when that money will run out.

For example, a man we will call Frank chose to reverse mortgage his home so that he could stay in the house and put food on the table. And now he has two years left before his property will be depleted of equity. He's in his nineties and because he doesn't have enough money saved to cover the taxes on the property he no longer owns, he is at risk of being homeless. How sad is that?

I don't want you to worry about having to dip into your principal. Let's position you to live off the interest of your investments and fund your financial freedom. And if you can do that, you won't be dependent on the government. (Will Social Security be around when you need it? Your guess is as good as mine.)

So how much can you take out of your investment accounts before you're depleting your principal? According to the Trinity study, which was really a category of studies designed to determine safe withdrawal rates, you can safely take out 4 percent of your investment balance each year without affecting the compound interest.

I'm not going to get into the ups and downs of it all, because that's too much math for me. This 4 percent rule may not really be 4 percent when you take all the variables into account, like interest rate fluctuations, market swings, and the shifting value of money each year, for example. Do you remember when gumballs cost a penny? Me neither.

No perfect scenario can generate perpetual income forever. But for all intents and purposes, if you can live entirely off 4 percent interest, you've reached financial freedom. When you make 4 percent of your savings a doable number to support your life, you can live off that money for a very, very long time. But how much money do you need in your investment accounts to earn enough interest to live on? Do you need a million each year? Maybe $100,000?

Here's another simple percentage rule to help you figure this out: the 75 percent rule. When you can live off interest only and are in the golden years, expect to live on 75 percent of your current annual income. The reason you can live on less in the later stages of life is you will likely have fewer expenses. You (hopefully) don't have to pay for big life events, like weddings. Your kids are grown and (hopefully) supporting themselves. Most or all your loans are (hopefully) paid off. You may own a home outright or its market value has increased while you have chipped away at the mortgage. Remember Parkinson's Law: With more, you spend more, and with less, you adjust to living on less. Plus, with most of your big spends in your rearview mirror, you may not even notice.

So let's say your household makes $70,000 a year right now. You'll likely be able to live off $52,500 a year just as comfortably in the future. To be clear, I'm not trying to rain on your parade. If you want your future self to live large, go ahead and plan for that goal. I'm just saying if you can live off $70,000 today, living off $52,500 in the near future will be a piece of cake. Red velvet cake, ideally.

The psychology around the 75 percent rule is about loss aversion. Once we are used to living a certain lifestyle, we want to maintain it. The drive to sustain what we have is much greater than the drive to get to the next level. Meaning, we will do anything to keep what we have because the pain of losing it is too great. That's how Frank ended up reverse-mortgaging his house. He didn't want to face downsizing from his four-bedroom home into a smaller home or an apartment, even though he didn't need all the space.

I understand why Frank didn't want to move. I love my home and lifestyle too, and the thought of having to scale back is almost unbearable. That's why I'm determined to work hard to maintain it, even if it means compromising my most precious resource: time. This instinct, driven by loss aversion, is deeply ingrained in all of us. To counteract it, we need a strategy that allows us to avoid loss in the future, one that ensures we can sustain the life we enjoy today without fear or sacrifice.

If you want to maintain your lifestyle in retirement, what's your investment goal? Let's break it down. We have concluded that living off $70,000 a year today means you want your investments to generate $52,500 annually, without dipping into your savings. That means building a portfolio large enough to yield $52,500 in interest alone.

ANNUAL SAVINGS WITHDRAWAL GOAL

Desired Annual Income	Principal Required (Average Yield 4%)
$25,000	$625,000
$50,000	$1,250,000
$75,000	$1,875,000
$100,000	$2,500,000
$250,000	$6,250,000
$500,000	$12,500,000
$1,000,000	$25,000,000
$5,000,000	$125,000,000

Annual savings withdrawal goal. Determine your desired annual income and estimate how much you will need in savings to live off interest alone.

You can see from this chart that if you want to withdraw $52,500 from your investments every year (without eating away at the principal), you'll need a balance of over $1.25 million. Now that you have that number, look at the savings goal charts earlier in this chapter to figure out how much you need to start saving now to reach this investment goal by the time you want to achieve it.

Let's assume you need an investment balance of $1.25 million within twenty-five years if you want to live off interest alone. In the chart, we see that $1.25 million yields an annual income of $50,000, so to hit your target you will need a slightly bigger chunk of savings.

In the savings goals charts, we can estimate that to save $1 million in twenty-five years, requires contributions of $402.19 every week. But that gets you "only" to $1 million in savings and we are targeting $1.25 million, so you need a bit more than that. You can get the exact number from the free resources at, say it with me, mymoneyhabit.com.

Use This Shortcut

Here's the ultimate Money Habit shortcut to determine how much of your current income to save annually to live financially free. This shortcut applies the 75 percent rule for the income you will want to sustain annually and the 4 percent rule for the interest you can take without affecting your principal. We are also assuming a 4.75 percent return on your investments, which compound.

- Financially free in five years—Save 325 percent of your current income annually. This requires a significant windfall (thanks, Grandma) or major sacrifice (like working three jobs to get your total income up 3.25 times your current level).
- Financially free in ten years—Save 150 percent of your current income annually. This goal is extreme, but slightly more achievable than doing it in five years, and likely achievable only when money falls in your lap or you get a rockstar income raise.
- Financially free in twenty-five years—Save 39 percent of your current income annually. This goal requires you to be hardcore in saving your pennies, but it's doable.
- Financially free in fifty years—Save 9 percent of your current income annually. This goal is very achievable and realistic for most people.

Let's break this down with a current income of $100,000:

- Twenty-five-year goal—If you want to earn $75,000 annually in interest twenty-five years from today, you'll need to save 39 percent of your income ($39,000) each year.
- Fifty-year goal—If your goal is to earn $75,000 in annual interest within fifty years, you'll need to save just 9 percent of your income ($9,000) annually.

For households with higher incomes, the same principles apply. For instance, if your household income is $250,000 and you aim for financial freedom within twenty-five years with an annual income goal of $187,500 (75 percent of $250,000), you'll need to save 39 percent, or $97,500, annually. If your goal is within fifty years, you'll need to save approximately 9 percent, or $22,500, annually.

By using this shortcut and starting early, you make financial freedom a realistic and achievable goal. Remember, the key is consistency and leveraging the power of compounding.

My goal is not to overwhelm you or, God forbid, have you throw your hands up in the air and give up. I want to show you that time is your friend; the earlier you start, the better. I also want to point out those windfall moments, like when Grandma passes, and she leaves behind her cherished apple pie recipe and a chunk of change. Any unexpected money you come into is an opportunity to sprint forward in your financial freedom journey. Invest it, save it, and you'll compress the time you need to live off interest alone. I think Grandma wants you to have freedom from financial worry more than a new car. Plus, who needs new wheels when you are regularly feasting on the world's best apple pie?

Your Most Precious Resource

One morning, while on a trip to Arizona, my friend Rich Manders and I decided to hike Camelback Mountain, the famous peak in the Scottsdale area. Rich is an incredible guy. He's an accomplished athlete; he's completed five Ironman Triathlon races and counting. (Not bad for sixty. Heck, not bad for anyone of any age.) He's built a life filled with love, family, and purpose. And he is financially free.

As we hiked up the mountain at a strong pace, my heart pounding out of my chest, we started talking about money and life. At one point, Rich stopped, turned to me, placed his hand on my shoulder, and said something I'll never forget:

"There comes a day for every person when time becomes permanently more valuable than money. Make sure your money is addressed before that moment, so you can focus all your energy on what forever will matter most: time."

Rich's words landed. My heart slowed and I took it all in. Then he turned and jogged up the trail. Yes, he jogged *up* a mountain.

You may have noticed, in the previous section, I didn't ask you to think about how much you would need to fund your retirement. I asked you to fund your financial freedom. The reason is that retirement has historically been associated with a person's age. At the time of this writing in the United States, retirement happens when you turn sixty-seven, or whatever seemingly random number society assigns. Waiting for retirement seems like we are programmed to chug along to hit that magic age and suddenly stop working.

I have a different perspective on this, and a different set of goals. Rather than focus on the day I won't have to work, I focus on achieving financial freedom, so I don't *have* to work. And because I'm also committed to doing the work that gives me purpose and joy, I may choose to keep working long after "official retirement age."

Let's be real. I will probably be writing books and trying to help folks like you and me for many years to come, because I'm on a mission, and that mission gives me energy. I may slow down so I can spend more time with my wife and family, but I'm not going to cash it all in on some government-appointed magical day. Not a chance.

My dad followed the traditional retirement script. At sixty-four, he left work, taking what his company called early retirement. For a few years, he enjoyed the time freedom; playing golf, traveling, and relaxing. But I vividly remember him eventually saying, "Many days are empty. I have nothing to do."

My father, who was an engineer, was basically *Star Trek*'s Spock minus the pointy ears and awkwardly tight uniform. He had expected, based on actuarial tables, to live until about seventy-five. Instead, he lived twenty years beyond that. Financially, he was comfortable, living off the interest from his investments. Before he passed, he ensured my mom was provided for, and she has continued to live off that interest. As I write this, she is ninety-one years old living comfortably in the house I was raised in.

My dad made the time/money inversion, which bionic Rich told me about, very abruptly at age sixty-four. Others do it more gradually. Some do it sooner; others, later. But all of us will come to the moment where time is the most precious thing. And it is a shame if, when that happens, we don't get fulfillment from it.

As William Penn, the founder of Pennsylvania, said, "Time is what we want most, but what, alas! we use worst." Don't let that be you. Your financial freedom empowers time freedom. And the best way to experience time freedom is through meaningful activity, something that brings you purpose and fulfillment. The ultimate win is making money while experiencing joy. And when your paychecks stop, let's make sure your finances are secure. Most importantly, may you always use your most precious resource, time, in the ways that matter most to you.

GET 'ER DONE SUMMARY
INVEST IN YOUR FUTURE YOU.

1 **Know where you are going.** Visit mymoneyhabit.com and use the free calculator and AI tools to figure out how much you need to save to hit your financial freedom number.

2 **Fund your Future You account.** Allocate money specifically for skill-building, courses, certifications, or anything that makes future you stronger, smarter, or more valuable.

3 **Set up an automatic investment.** Choose a small, consistent amount you can invest regularly (daily, weekly, or when you get paid). Use index funds and dollar-cost averaging. Let compounding do the work.

8

Embrace Your New Identity

THE FIRST TIME it happened, I didn't think anything of it.

We were shopping for new linen for our bed, and as we approached the checkout line, Krista wandered away. After I finished paying, she was right there to help me pack up the pillowcases, bed sheets, and such.

It happened again. And again. We'd get in line to pay, or approach a cashier, and she'd suddenly find something "interesting" to look at nearby. She wouldn't bolt, like, "See ya!" It was more casual, like she genuinely wanted to read everything about whatever product she found nearby. Could gum really be that fascinating? What's the deal?

When I asked her about it, she had no idea she'd been doing it. My curiosity led to a deep conversation that helped me understand more about her feelings about money. Years later, we talked about it again for this book.

"Once I started to become aware of what I was doing," Krista said, "I realized I was feeling panic. When we'd walk up to pay, my heart rate would accelerate, and I would start to feel hot. And I would start to feel shame. I was preparing myself to have everybody look at me and feel sorry for me. Or to think, 'Who is this loser?'"

Krista and I grew up differently. My mother still lives in the house I grew up in. Krista moved so much as a kid that she had to be prepared to pack her stuff in a garbage bag and be out in thirty minutes. I never worried about where our next meal would come from; I didn't even think about it. Krista had a lot of food insecurity. She still gets hives and shakes when recalling the humiliation of being sent to a separate cafeteria line for children who couldn't afford school lunch. The pain was so intense she often skipped lunch, the only nutritious meal she might have had that day. Where I took a full shopping cart for granted, Krista knew the sting of her mom coming up short at the register.

Krista said, "I was carrying around all those emotions with absolutely no awareness that I was doing it, because it such a part of my formative years, it was part of me."

When Krista was twelve, she severely injured her knee as a catcher during a softball game, colliding with a runner sliding into home. She broke her patella, tore her meniscus, and shredded her ACL. The diagnosis came from a chiropractor with an X-ray machine, her mother's only option. A hairstylist without health insurance, her mom bartered haircuts for ongoing chiropractic care. Chiropractic adjustments for torn cartilage? Broken bones? A shredded ACL? It was all they could do. Krista never received proper medical attention, and the injury became a lifelong burden.

Maybe you can relate. The consequences of financial trauma linger. Even in moments of joy, like our honeymoon to Disney World, her anxiety resurfaced. By Wednesday of any week-long trip that started on Saturday, she'd start trembling, convinced the money would run out, just as it always had in her childhood. For Krista, midway through any journey was as far as life would let her go. Wednesdays became a harbinger of collapse.

Three months ago, during Thanksgiving, Krista suffered severe burns when boiling water spilled on her foot. The pain was agonizing, but she refused medical attention, or even basic supplies like bandages or burn salve. Despite her delirium, she rejected every effort our children and I made to help. Against her protests, we bought the necessary supplies and, after days of convincing, she finally agreed to visit urgent care. Even with money in the bank, she couldn't justify using it. The circumstance didn't feel "worthy." Her mother's voice echoed in her mind: *Are you sure it's that bad?* Money was for survival, and even a severe burn didn't seem as critical as food for the night.

When we later talked about it, Krista acknowledged the root of her resistance. Growing up with no money meant accepting and expecting suffering. Even when there's a way to fix things, guilt and doubt creep in. *Does this qualify?* That's the insidious imprint of financial trauma. It warps your ability to care for yourself or others, even when the solution is sitting, waiting for you, in a well-funded bank account.

Krista and I talked at length about sharing her story with you. It's exposing, raw, and painful to relive. We deliberated, and we agreed to share it under two conditions. First, that it serves you in your own journey, to know that if you've experienced financial trauma, you or your loved ones are not alone. Second, Krista wants you to know one thing: She got the runner out at home plate. *#WorthIt**

As we worked the Money Habit system over the years, we started having more conversations about money, and our feelings around money. Over time, the system gave her the feeling of safety she had craved since she was a child, but it took time to get used to that feeling. "I think not opening bills was part of my mom's survival," Krista said. "So it was hard for me to develop a relationship with money where I understood that knowing is your freedom."

Change happened, but slowly.

I remember playing basketball at the local high school one day and landing awkwardly after a jump shot, badly twisting my ankle.

---

* Krista insisted I include *#WorthIt*. She can be a bit competitive. And a small part of her hopes that girl she tagged out at home plate is reading this and is reminded that *she was out*!

As I limped home, all I could think about was how angry Krista would be when I told her I needed to see a doctor. At the time, I didn't understand why an injury would upset her so much. Life happens. People get hurt. Things can be fixed.

We had just started our Money Habit, and in Krista's world things couldn't just be "fixed." Her anger stemmed from fear, the constant reverberating question *Does this qualify?* But as the system took hold, those feelings of fear and anger started to fade. New emotions took their place, ones neither of us expected. Ultimately, it was a pair of red-bottomed shoes that signified a new reality of control, confidence, and safety.

That shift from anger, fear, and endless questioning didn't happen overnight. It took years. But now, Krista doesn't panic at cash registers. She doesn't walk away because she suddenly feels the need to compare prices on groceries or something else. "I still feel it," she told me. "It still hurts me. It still feels like part of my DNA. But now I am the master over it. It's no longer the master of me.

"Just being aware of my feelings and where they come from is half the battle," Krista continued. "I remind myself, 'I'm feeling this way because of how I grew up. Is that happening right now? No. I'm okay. I've got this.' That was a huge awakening for me, the power in knowing this is exactly how much I have to spend, and I can act accordingly. I can act in the greater good for me, and for our family, and for whatever is happening. *That* is where the safety lives. Realizing that was life-changing for me."

The Money Habit system works because it does not ask you to change. But if you work the Money Habit system, it will change *you*.

Now You Can Talk About Money

Talking about money in many households can feel like navigating a minefield. One wrong step, a question about spending or savings, and the evening (or the week) could implode. Maybe you've been there.

It can start innocently enough with a question like, "Can we afford that?" but may quickly spiral into blame, defensiveness, or icy silence. Unsurprisingly, money is one of the top reasons couples argue, according to research from the American Psychological Association.

It doesn't have to be this way.

Who manages the money in your household? If you live with someone, is it a shared effort, or does one person handle the finances while the other stays in the dark?

Rachel Werner, one of our personal finance experts who coaches couples through the Money Habit system, observed distinct patterns in her work. "In most relationships," she explained, "one person takes the lead on finances, while the other often feels like an outsider, or worse, like a child being given or denied permission. These dynamics create frustration and resentment on both sides."

Krista and I lived through this ourselves. Back then, our money conversations were, shall we say, lively. Krista would ask, "Mike, do we have enough for groceries?"

My response, classic in its unhelpfulness, would be something like, "How much do you plan to spend?" On the surface, it seemed like an exchange of facts, but it was laced with the subtext of blame. I interpreted her question as a lack of planning, and Krista heard my response as an accusation that she was being frivolous. The conversation would spiral from there. "How the hell should I know?" would meet "How the hell don't you know?" until we fell into an icy silence.

You and I both know it wasn't about the groceries. It was about clarity, or the lack of it. Without clarity, money discussions become minefields of guesswork and misunderstanding.

The Money Habit system changed everything for us. I still take the lead in managing allocations and paying bills, but Krista is fully engaged. Whenever she wants, she logs into the accounts and immediately sees what's available: what we have for groceries, a date night, or a splurge she's been considering. If a balance looks tight, she might say, "Mike, it looks like we've got a situation in the

N-Groceries account, want to take a peek?" No accusations. No drama. Just clarity.

Now, instead of playing the parent and child, we're partners. The system takes on the "bad guy" role when necessary, delivering the hard truths with cold, impartial numbers. Our conversations shifted from "Can we afford this?" to "What should we prioritize?" What used to end in icy silence now feels like a cozy, warm collaboration.

Rachel Werner saw this transformation in the couples she coached in the Money Habit system. One husband, who had previously felt disconnected from financial decisions, shared: "For the first time, I feel like I have authority over my hobbies. I don't have to ask permission anymore."

Another couple described how their conversations went from finger-pointing to focusing on shared goals. As Rachel explained, "When the system provides clarity, it replaces emotional tension with progress and positivity."

Kelly Ruta is my go-to expert for people struggling with the mindset around money. Kelly is a no BS, "let's get results" psychotherapist and behavior expert who dove into why this system works.

"At the root of many money conflicts," Kelly said, "is a clash between control and autonomy. When one partner feels they have to 'report' to the other, or when financial decisions are made in a vacuum, it stokes defensiveness, resentment, and shame. But when both people have clarity and autonomy within a shared framework, those emotional triggers diminish."

There's that rebel nature again, the stuff psychologist Howard Farkas discovered on why people cave in to emotional eating habits, which we talked about in chapter 1. Seems we can't help ourselves! We've just got to be free!

Krista's journey with money has also evolved. Traditional budgeting used to amplify her fear of not having enough, but with the Money Habit system, she always knows exactly what's available without crunching through spreadsheets or financial systems. There's no guesswork, no need to ask for approval or avoid conversations out of anxiety.

This clarity isn't just practical; it's transformative. Krista once told me, "If something ever happened to you, Mike, I need to know how to handle everything. And now I feel I can." That conversation stuck with me. Financial transparency isn't just about the present; it's about equipping your partner to navigate the future with confidence.

Money conversations don't have to be heavy or stressful. With a clear system in place, they can be simple check-ins, celebrations of progress, or collaborative planning sessions. If you've been avoiding money talks, start small. Sit down with your partner this week, log into your accounts together, and look at the balances. What do the numbers tell you? Are there areas to adjust or goals to celebrate?

> ☑ **TAKE QUICK ACTION**
> Schedule a "money meeting" (I love alliteration) with your partner. It doesn't have to be formal. Pour a couple of coffees, sit down at the kitchen table, and talk about what you see. Let the system guide your discussion. As you do this regularly, you'll notice that clarity replaces confusion, and collaboration takes the place of conflict. A bonus discovery: When you can talk about money, you can talk about anything.

When Your Partner Doesn't Want to Participate

Sometimes, one person in a relationship is ready to take control of their money, and the other, well, isn't. Maybe they're skeptical, overwhelmed, or just tired of yet another "system." Maybe they've had bad experiences in the past, or maybe they don't even realize how unsafe money conversations feel to them. Whatever the reason, a partner's resistance isn't a permanent roadblock. It's usually a sign they don't feel safe, empowered, or included in the process. That's where your leadership, not pressure, comes in.

Maggie Reyes is a marriage coach and the host of *The Marriage Life Coach Podcast*. When I interviewed her for this book, she said something that stuck with me: "When couples struggle to communicate about money, almost every communication problem is really a safety problem." It's not as much about the numbers as it is about how the conversations happen. So start by creating emotional safety.

That doesn't mean ambushing them for a budget beat down. It means soft starts. Transparency. Asking for input. Acknowledging frustrating finances. Giving them room to consider.

One client of Maggie's used this approach and was shocked when her ultrapractical husband responded not with frustration but with his own spreadsheet, because she'd given him space to think, not react.

If your partner still doesn't engage? That's okay. You start. You don't need a big announcement, and you don't need permission. Just begin managing your side of the finances with clarity and consistency. Set up your accounts, stick to your categories, and let the results speak for themselves.

As Kelly Ruta put it, "Your motivation can't be getting a specific reaction." You're not doing this to change them; you're doing it because it's who you want to be. Maggie Reyes agrees, and explained that, often, when one person leads with calm and clarity, the other follows. Not always immediately, but eventually.

And if they never want to participate? Then the system still works. You can still gain peace, clarity, and control for yourself. And over time, you might get closer, or you might get clearer. But no matter what, you'll get stronger. Because the truth is, the Money Habit system isn't just about finances; it's about stepping into who you are, and who you're becoming. You don't need to change your partner to change your financial life. You just need to start.

When Other People See You Differently

The last time I heard from Carol Piper, she was drinking a tropical drink and smiling big for the camera, with lush green mountains behind her. The email read: "In Costa Rica with sister for the next month. Gonna head back to my condo later tonight to do some remote work."

After that, she seemed to drop off the face of the earth.

Carol was in the first group of Profit First Professionals: accounting, bookkeeping, and financial services pros who are certified to help people implement Profit First. I worked with her personally, and I coached her and a few other people on an early version of the Money Habit system. I remember asking her about her vision for financial independence. Carol said, "I'll know I have arrived when I have a vacation condo in Costa Rica, near my sister. I want to go there, have my own place to stay, and spend time with my family. That's my dream."

We assessed Carol's income and allocations, set up her accounts (we called them "buckets" at the time), removed wasteful spending, and increased her income with extra projects. Within a few years of using the Money Habit system, Carol had saved enough money to buy her vacation home.

About four months later, I started hearing from other people in the Money Habit group that she hadn't been around. They met monthly to hold each other accountable and offer strategy and support, and, since buying her condo, she'd missed all the meetings and hadn't responded to emails, phone calls, or texts from other members. Carol seemed to be active online, so they knew she was physically safe, but why had she ghosted them?

A few months later, the story came out. Carol lost her condo. She was back home in Kansas, and she was struggling financially. We heard through the grapevine that her old friends had given her a lot of attitude about the positive changes she'd made. They had been telling her, "Oh, so you're rich now. You think you're better than us." They gave her a hard time about her "new friends" (the Money Habit group) and her new life.

The pressure to hang on to her old identity, the life she knew, was too great. So Carol started pulling away from the group that shared her new beliefs and goals. Eventually, she abandoned her new friends so she could hang on to her old gang.

Sometimes, when we improve ourselves, people in our lives give us crap about it. And if we're already feeling uncomfortable in our new reality, that could be enough to cause us to revert to our old ways, the habits and routines that matched our old expectations of ourselves. That's what Carol did. She let go of her new money habits so she could keep her old life. Eventually, she sold her condo in Costa Rica at a loss. So not only did she kill her dream, but also she ended up deeper in debt.

The people who truly care about you will show up for your new life. They'll be proud of you and supportive of you; they'll stick around. And the more financially free you become, the more people you'll find who share your values and goals. Besides, anyone with half a brain knows it's a good thing when your friend gets a condo in Costa Rica. I mean, free vacation, right?

Be aware of whom you surround yourself with. They influence your money habits more than you know.

A Pair of Really Expensive Shoes

My wife is one of the best-dressed people I know, a true fashionista. She loves a bargain and has an incredible ability to put together stunning outfits on any budget. For years, she dreamed of owning a pair of Christian Louboutin shoes: glossy black high heels with signature red bottoms that reveal their elegance with every step. They are unmistakable and they are expensive: $800 for a pair.

Krista bought them.

She told me how, for years, the idea of buying something like this had been unthinkable. In her formative experience with money, buying shoes like these was more than a no—it was shameful. Spending in one area always meant taking from another. *Shoes could mean no rent for our apartment. Fixing a broken knee could mean no food for our family.* Every decision carried the weight of a trade-off, that constant calculation of *Does this qualify?*

But with our Money Habit system, life was different. Before she made the purchase, she checked her "slush fund," the W-Krista's

Debit account. The money was sitting there, specifically allocated for moments like this. When she approached the cash register, her heart raced and her thoughts whirled, but not out of fear. This time, there was no worry she was taking from something or someone else. No anxiety about whether the purchase qualified. The system had already answered that question. The racing heart and whirling thoughts were anticipation, excitement, thrill.

In that moment, Krista experienced her turning point to financial independence. Yours is coming too. Ironically, financial independence isn't about how much you make or save; it's about having every dollar accounted for, without needing to do any mental gymnastics. The money takes care of itself. You know exactly what can be done now, what is coming your way, and what needs to wait. You know that you're never taking from something or someone else. You know what "qualifies."

For the first time, Krista felt what it was like to spend without guilt, fully confident that everything else was secure. The cashier asked, "Would you like me to wrap these?"

"That's not necessary," she said with a smile. "I have another idea."

And with that, she walked out of the store in those Christian Louboutin heels. *#WorthIt*

GET 'ER DONE SUMMARY
CHANGE THE CONVERSATION; CHANGE EVERYTHING.

1 **Schedule a "money meeting" with your partner.** Sit down at the kitchen table and log in to your Money Habit bank accounts together. Look at what's there. Talk about it. Let the system, not your assumptions, guide the conversation. This one small habit turns confusion (or conflict) into clarity and commitment.

Conclusion
Go Get Your Moments

IMAGINE YOU wake up one morning and hear a ringing sound in your ear, like you went to a way-too-loud concert the night before. Now imagine that sound is constant, a squealing note that never pauses and never ends. You hear the ringing under everything: music, fire alarms, the sound of your own voice. And the sound is loudest when your surroundings are the quietest. You hear it every millisecond of your conscious life. That is tinnitus, a condition I've had since birth.

The high-pitched ringing sound is with me in every moment, in conversations, on stage when I'm giving speeches, when I am alone with my thoughts, as I write this to you right now. I can't will the sound to go away, or meditate it away, or drown it out. I *can* redirect my attention so I'm not fixating on the sound as much, but it's always there in the background of my life. This is why I use background music whenever the opportunity presents itself. The music doesn't drown out the sound, but it pulls my attention away from it.

The funny thing about tinnitus is I had no idea I had it. I thought everyone heard the ringing sound. You, me. Shoot, I assumed mosquitoes even had it, if they could hear. I assumed everyone and everything heard the ring. When in actuality about 5 percent of the world population has chronic tinnitus, like I do.

When I was in my thirties, I was hiking through the woods with my friend Mark and he said, "It's so quiet."

I said, "Yeah... just the ring."

Mark had no idea what I was talking about.

Do you know Simon & Garfunkel's moody song "The Sound of Silence"? When I first heard it, I was convinced they were talking about the actual sound of silence; you know, the ring. That must be the sound, right? I have never experienced total silence at any point in my life. I can't even fathom it.

When I tell people about the droning in my head, they assume it's a struggle for me, that it's nature's version of torture. New technology is becoming available that could reduce the squeal, maybe eradicate it. My audiologist proposed the process to me. He thinks it may cure the "maddening" sound I hear. Every time he mentions it to me, I have declined. I don't know any other way.

The droning is part of me; it's just who I am. In a way, the uncomfortable sound is comfortable; I've learned to live with it. I have accepted it, and that I will never really know what the hell Paul Simon and Art Garfunkel mean by "the sound of silence."

For most of us, money is an uncomfortable topic and managing it is an uncomfortable task. But this discomfort feels normal. The financial struggle is like that droning, an ever-constant sound. It becomes so ingrained in us that it feels normal, almost comforting. You're used to it. Maybe you even get a little rush when you find the money for an overdue bill or solve some other financial crisis. Yes, worrying about money is stressful. But you don't know any other way. It's part of you. It's just who you are. In a way, the uncomfortable feeling is comfortable.

The financial struggle was like that for me too. I didn't grow up with that worry, but from the moment I went out on my own after college, I was in it. I had my own young and growing family, so the pressure was on and it stayed on, for decades.

I can divert my attention from the ringing sound by using tricks to temporarily forget about it, but it's always there. I do it so often that it is subconscious. Music will always be playing in the background if I can access it. Tapping a table with my hand works a bit, but I found that annoys other people. Know what makes noise for me, but you can't hear? Clicking my teeth together. I am so good at it, that I can do it without anyone noticing. It's not a distraction for anyone, but what a wonderful temporary reprieve from the squeal for me.

We do the same thing with money too, right? We distract ourselves from the discomfort with impulse buys, television, social media, whatever it takes.

You can use countless tricks to ignore it or dodge the money discomfort for a bit. You can go to the movies with your friends, focus on work throughout the day, go for an adventure with your kids, but that financial struggle is still a relentless undercurrent. A constant, annoying drone that makes you feel as though you are just months, or weeks, or even days away from a financial crisis and the fear that the *next* crisis will be the one you won't be able to handle.

Before I started using the system that would become The Money Habit, my financial worries consumed me. And because I was so freaked out about impending crises, I did the only thing I knew to do: work more to bring in more. If I could just finally, once and for all, make enough money, I wouldn't have to worry. Except, when you don't have a system to manage your money, there's never enough. So, the worries drone on, and on, and on.

Because I was always trying to make more money to provide for my family and keep my business running, I worked all the time. All. The. Time. And because I prioritized work, I missed a lot of important moments with my family. I almost never attended my kids' sporting or school events if they were scheduled on weekdays, and I also missed weekends if I had the opportunity to make money. The money worry was urgent, more "important," and so Krista attended the kids' events without me. My worry was bigger than my want. I *wanted* to go, but I worried about money more. So I told myself I couldn't go. That I had to sacrifice life's moments to hopefully have future moments when I finally earned enough.

On the weekends, when I did make it to a game, I wasn't really there. The ringing thoughts of working more to make more to cover the next thing was incessant. I'd be hanging with people I love but I was only half there. This was true for years. Decades, actually. I missed so many moments because I was checked out or couldn't be there at all. Long after I got our money challenges under control and we were using the Money Habit system, I still clung to the work mode, because it was part of me. The drone of make, make, make was the new normal. It was all I knew.

The moments ticked by, and before I knew it, our youngest, Jake, was a senior in high school.

Krista called me one day and said, "Hey, can you come to Jake's final track meet?"

Immediately, my mind went to default mode. I started to say, "I'm sorry, I'm so busy," but my heart screamed, "Go to the @#$%! meet. This is your literal last shot. Go. To. The. Meet."

I went.

Leaning against the fence around the field, holding hands with Krista, I noticed so many parents and several other couples. I thought, *That's pretty miraculous, to devote time to this, in the middle of the workday! Doesn't everyone have to work? Doesn't everyone hear the drone, the need to make more money?*

And then Jake came around the corner, running as hard as he could. He spotted me and his face lit up like it was Christmas. His gait changed, and he pushed even harder. He seemed almost cocky, like he was showing off and thinking, *My dad's here, my dad's here.*

In that moment, in *that present moment,* I became overwhelmed with the joy of watching him run. As he ran the final section, I thought, this sliver of time is majestic. I don't recall where Jake placed in the race. But for me this was the winning moment! I don't know if he remembers that day, but I'll never forget it.

On the drive home, I thought, *Holy cow. That's the first time I've been truly present in years. I'd robbed myself and the people I love of my presence.* And I'd robbed myself of so much joy. Once I got a taste of it, I wanted more. I wanted all of it, all the moments. And I want that for you too.

The constant droning worry didn't just cause me to miss important moments. Sometimes, it got worse *in the moment*, like when Krista would order a glass of nice wine at dinner, and I'd start freaking out about the bill. She would feel ashamed and embarrassed that I got uncomfortable, and the evening would be ruined. I can't even count the number of times my fixation about how much money we were spending on dinner, or movie popcorn, or whatever prevented me from enjoying our time together.

But the moment I started using the Money Habit system for myself, I got better at being present, enjoying the moment, and giving my family my undivided attention. It wasn't long before I was able to do that no matter the circumstance. I made this change not because I had more money or was making more. I made this change because I knew what money was available for what purpose, before I spent a dime. You see, I no longer worried about the money, because the system gave me a set of instructions about what I could or couldn't do with the money. Alas, my worry (and yours) is rooted in uncertainty.

I mentioned this concept earlier in the book, but it is worth repeating: Not knowing is the greatest cause of anxiety and worry for humans. According to Uncertainty Theory, people often experience higher anxiety while waiting for results, such as during a breast biopsy, than they do after receiving a confirmed cancer diagnosis.

In other words, people feel more comfort hearing "You have cancer" than "You *may* have cancer."

Experts suggest that once a diagnosis is known, even if it's serious, patients can begin to act and make informed decisions, which alleviates anxiety. And that is what The Money Habit did for me. The day I started using it, I knew my diagnosis, and I have never stopped knowing it since. Sometimes it is good, sometimes it is bad, and occasionally it is ugly. But the worry of not knowing is gone and I can take action.

The constant churn of money worries is a loss of freedom—emotional freedom. You're not free to be fully engaged with your life when the undercurrent is always, *How are we going to get by?* You may not even realize that "ringing sound" is always with you, droning away. Because you're used to it. It's part of you. It's just who you are.

But it doesn't have to be. You can be free to live in the moment. To enjoy your life. To be fully engaged with the people you love and the things you love to do. To go out for dinner and not worry about the check. To take time off from work to celebrate your mom on her birthday. To have fun even if things go wrong, because you're not worried about how much the "wrong" will cost. To spend an afternoon in nature, or listening to your kids make up songs, or exploring something you love without worrying that you should be doing something more productive. To live into who you were always meant to be.

I don't want you to miss the moments anymore. I *beg* you not to miss the moments. I want you to have *all* the moments and be *emotionally present* for all of them.

And now you know how to do that. You have learned a proven system that will free you from the ever-present worry about money for the first time in your life. You know how to customize the Money Habit system to suit your life and goals. And you know how to adjust it when you shift into a new financial season. You've got tools, and skills, and clarity. And you've already started taking action.

I titled this book *The Money Habit* because humanity is wired a certain way. We're built to accumulate, portion, and consume. Early humans foraged for food, stored it for later, and ate portions when hunger dictated so. That instinct to collect, divide, and distribute is hardwired into everyone. It is exactly how *you* are hardwired.

And these same principles apply to your finances. If you are uncomfortable with money, that's nature's call for correction. If you are regularly uncomfortable, that's her decree for correction. We need to fix that before we accept it as "just the way things are." They aren't.

Being at ease about money will feel odd at first. I get that. It's like having tinnitus. There's an invention that could be a cure for it: a haptic bracelet that eradicates the condition. Every time you notice the sound, it vibrates, and that vibration trains your brain to stop hearing the sound. I can't even imagine it! In fact, I'm nervous about it. Scared, even. What does total silence sound like? I'm not sure I want to know. Part of me doesn't want to lose the ringing sound because I'm afraid. Who will I be without it? What if I can't go back?

We cling to financial struggle in the same way. We're used to it. It's part of us. It's just who we are.

This morning Krista reminded me, "Do you remember when Adayla gave you her piggy bank? Those years were dark, but I felt oddly comforted. I told myself, *I've been here before. I know how to handle having nothing. Just focus on tomorrow. Survive just one more day. Each day.*"

She was ready to return to that place, not because it was better, but because it was what she knew. Bad can feel good when it's all you've ever known.

But I, she, and now you know there's another way. You've already experienced it. And with the Money Habit system, you don't have to change who you are. The system works because it works with your habits.

In the silence, in the absence of worry, there is only the present moment.

Who will you be now, in this present moment?

Without the constant churn and stress of getting by, what is possible for you? What moments do you want to experience? And with whom? And doing what?

You have enough money, but you may not have enough moments. Go get them. Stack them up. Stack all the moments up and live them fully. Give them to the people you love. Give them to yourself. Collect the moments and keep them with you.

Being present in your life, that is a present for you, and that present is priceless.

You don't have to accept the money problems that have been a constant in your life. It isn't even "normal." The freedom you will have, which you can't even imagine right now, will change your life in so many positive ways. I promise. In the absence of worry, in your own ease, you will become who you were always meant to be. It will be awkward at first. You may even worry because you are not worried, or that it's only temporary and the "other shoe will drop" at any moment. It's okay. You are ready.

You are ready to live fully in the moment.

As I write these final words, I feel like you are speaking to me, from the future. I know that makes no sense with time and space. But I also feel this need to go for freedom. Freedom from the squeal. I am off to make a call and schedule an appointment for the haptic bracelet my audiologist wants me to use to extinguish my tinnitus. I'm excited and kind of scared. Tearing up a bit. Oh, my God. Maybe I can experience silence for the first time in my life.

Imagine that. You experience real financial freedom, perhaps for the first time in your life. And I will experience silence. We'll both be even more present, more in the moment.

If I ever have the privilege to meet you, let's make a vow. Nod and put one finger to your lip (that one that signifies quiet), and I will nod and do the same to you. Not a word said. Maybe just a single tear shed. In this way we will acknowledge each other, and the courage you had to step powerfully into a new life where you silenced the financial worry.

Oh, the sound of silence. That beautiful sound of silence.

Acknowledgments

THIS BOOK exists because of an extraordinary group of people who wake up every day determined to shift the very axis of this planet. One soul, one bank account, one life at a time. They aren't just devoted to this book; they are devoted to a healthier world for all of us. And it starts with financial stability.

Anjanette "AJ" Harper: You worked on this exhaustively. You were relentless and never quit, even with unbelievable life events swirling around you. You just kept showing up and got this done because it had to get done. Thank you for being more than a best friend. Thank you for being an extraordinary writing partner. I hope every aspiring (and established) author takes the time to listen to your sage wisdom on the *Don't Write That Book* podcast.

Trena White and Jesse Finkelstein: I've found my people. Kindness *does* win. I'm honored to be a Page Two author. You've built a community I've always longed for, and I'm proud to be part of it. And we have an imprint! Eek!

Andrea Conway: Thank you for your relentless commitment to the entire Michaloverse. This book is nothing without awareness, and you've devoted yourself to making sure *this* work is discovered because it *needs* to be. I wouldn't be surprised to see you actually shouting from the mountain tops.

Kelsey Ayres: You lead our organization with effortless grace and kindness, and because of you, our team is magnetized. I have never in my life worked at a company that has given me so much joy. Thank you for leading us and handling all the behind-the-scenes negotiations that make this possible.

Leslie Bootle: I deeply value your direct support in driving the marketing and circulation strategy for this book at Page Two. Your strategic insight, deep publishing expertise, and genuine dedication to this book's success made an impact from day one. And the bestest part... you're good people!

Rony Ganon: Thank you for leading the charge on this book's creation at Page Two. The management process has been nothing short of superb. Everything was measured, on time, and when flexibility was needed, you made it happen.

Kendra Ward: Your editing of this book was incredible. I love that you didn't just ensure clarity for the reader, you highlighted the highs and lows of this emotional journey. You saw where the giggles should land and where the tears should drop. That's the reality of finance, and I'm so happy you made sure it was reflected in the book.

Adrineh Der-Boghossian: Say that name five times fast, says the guy named Michael Michalowicz. You meticulously reviewed every calculation, citation, and concept in this book, correcting all the non-obvious issues I couldn't spot. Truly brilliant work!

Peter Cocking: I love the design work you put into this cover. You made sure it conveyed the real message of money: It's bright and optimistic, and needs to be protected. They say not to judge a book by its cover because people *do*. You made sure we're judged well and the book is opened.

To the Michaloverse A-Team: I'm consistently astonished by how much you accomplish and how deeply you care for our readers. My deepest thanks to **Erin Chazotte** for ensuring I am in the right place at the right time, doing the right thing. To **Adalya Michalowicz** for her incredible care of all our authors. To **Cordé Reed**, who does whatever it takes to serve our mission, which includes, apparently, overseeing the safe transport of my mom's lasagna. To **Jenna Lorenz** for writing prose that serves countless readers we may never have the privilege to meet. And last but not least, to the "momma" of our office, **Amy Cartelli**, who would adopt every member of our "whacky" and beautiful community if she could.

To my wife, Krista: Thank you for the conversations we had about money. Conversations that cracked open awareness, honesty, and healing. This book wouldn't be what it is without those conversations, and I know they'll never end. I live you (not a typo).

To my kids, Tyler, Adayla, and Jake: Here's to each of you marching forward on your own paths to financial independence. Watching you build your lives, your dreams, your futures, on your own terms, reminds me every day why this mission matters.

To my parents: Thank you for laying the foundation of financial health that I have returned to time and time again. Dad, I miss you. Mom, I see your strength. Thank you for showing me what it means to deeply care for others.

And finally, to you, the friend I hope to make one day: Thank you for reading this book. Now, go! Make your move. Shift your world. Heal your finances, once and for all. Your success will be another positive shift in our planet. Then, if you feel called, guide others to do the same. Their success will elevate us all.

Appendix
Tips and Hacks to Save More Money

Find and Manage Subscriptions

Subscriptions are the bane of the financially fit. They are the modern mini version of timeshares. According to C+R Research, the average American spends $219 per month on subscriptions. Let me do the math for you. That's $2,628 each year! It's so easy to fall into "subscription creep," where those ten- and twenty-dollar subscriptions start to add up to a hefty amount. What's worse is you can easily sign up once and then be on the nearly impossible to cancel auto-billing forever. We forget about the sock-of-the-month club and that rando streaming service we signed up for just to binge watch a show we didn't even like. I forgot we had signed up for a wine club on our trip to Napa until we had way too much wine in our house. (Nobody needs that much wine.)

Most subscriptions get buried in with regular credit card expenses, and we don't notice the charges. So, in good ol' Money Habit fashion, we first need to make you conscious and aware, and then give you control. So big tip number one, get a dedicated card for subscriptions.

Put all your subscriptions on one credit card. That way, the fees won't be buried among all your other payments and bills. This technique will clarify what you're spending your money on, and how much. I did this with all my subscriptions and was shocked at the over $400 a month I had been spending. Nearly five Gs for every lap around the sun! My God, that kind of money is a pretty good vacation every year. One of the subscriptions was for my Hydrow rowing machine, a forty-dollar monthly charge. I like to row, but damn that was rich, and I didn't even need it. Discovering how much I'd been paying for the service inspired me to use YouTube videos to get rowing, elliptical machine, and other cardio and weight exercises. A TV in my home gym for $250 now has all the videos and coaching in the world. No subscriptions. When I don't feel inspired, I just search "workout video that will inspire me," and boom! Instant and free access.

Here are a few other tips to help you find and manage subscriptions.

Subscription Pause

Pause your subscriptions for a month or two. Don't let them renew automatically, only manually. When the break is over, you'll have a clear sense of which services you truly missed and are worth keeping, and which ones you can cancel for good without a second thought. I bet you may even forget you "needed" them so badly before.

Report Your Card Missing

This is a bit extreme, but it works in those situations of analysis paralysis that I talked about in chapter 5. Call your credit card company and report your card missing or stolen. Your subscriptions will notify you that they can't charge your card. If you don't give them your new card number, the subscription will be canceled. Note that some credit card companies continue to allow your auto-pay bill charges to come through when issuing you a new number, so make sure you ask about this and confirm that any charge against your old card will be rejected.

Streaming Subscriptions

Start watch parties with your neighbors or friends. Whoever has the subscription hosts the party. Plus cook meals together. Camaraderie, shared meals, and fewer subscription costs. Boom!

Align Your Credit Cards With Your Habits

As you've learned, it's far easier to work *with* our habits rather than try to change them. Sometimes credit cards are just too tempting, and we need to set up other guardrails to make it easier to curb spending.

Here are a few different techniques to help you align your credit cards with your habits.

Use Debit Cards

The easiest way to handle overspending on credit cards is to use debit cards instead, because the pain of spending money is immediate. Just make sure you use a debit card that does not charge for transactions.

Cut Credit Card Limits

To prevent overspending, call your credit card company and ask them to lower your spending limits. Yeah, it is an atypical call, and the customer service rep (cough, salesperson or AI bot) on the other side of the line will try to prevent you from reducing your limit. Or at least will ask why. You can tell them: "That dude Mike Michalowicz told me I need to do this, sooo…" Or, you can have fun and say that you caught someone abusing your credit card and this will fix it. Then give them a dramatic pause and say, "and I am that someone." Pause again, this time for laughter, from no one. You're welcome.

Freeze Your Credit Reports

This is one of my personal favorites, since it both curbs spending and keeps you safer from identity thieves. Call each of the credit bureaus (Experian, Equifax, and TransUnion) and ask them to freeze your credit reports. Once this is done, no one—including you—can apply for credit in your name. You can unfreeze your credit reporting when you need to apply for a loan or a big purchase. Fair warning: Freezing and unfreezing your credit can be a nuisance, but in honor of channeling your habits and preventing you from taking on new debt, that is a good thing.

Hide Your Cards

Ask a trusted friend to hide your credit cards in your home. When you have a justified reason to use it, call your friend and explain the reason why you need it. Of course, if you're in panic mode, you could just tear apart your house; it's usually taped behind the TV or under the coffee table anyway.

Use a Lockbox with a Timer

Store your credit cards in a timer lockbox. Before you open it to take out your card, you have to wait for the preset timer of thirty or sixty minutes. You can't access the card until the timer runs out. This gives you a much-needed delay and time to think about using the card. Do you really need it? If not, reset the lock before it unlocks. Unnecessary spend averted!

Pay Your Minimum Payment Automatically

If you have a predictable minimum payment for your credit cards, set up an auto-payment to cover that minimum amount plus a small additional amount. That way, you avoid paying late fees and the risk of an interest rate increase. For example, if you typically have $1,000 of credit card debt at the end of each month, and the minimum payment is $50, set up an automatic payment for $25 each week, for a total of $100. Now you've made the minimum payment (and won't ever get spanked by a late fee) and an additional $50 toward paying down debt.

Beg, Borrow, or Deal

You might remember my friend Rich Manders. He is the person who taught me about the time-money inversion, which I shared with you in chapter 7. Rich has a vacation home in Vermont. When we were still in our Recover season, I wanted to give my family a nice vacation, but we didn't have enough in the DREAMS account to cover more than a weekend at a motel. So I called up Rich. "I'd like to ask you a favor. Please feel free to say, 'There's a conflict' or 'I can't right now' or simply no and you don't need to explain why. I want to give my family a vacation, and we don't have access to much money right now for that purpose. Is there ever any opportunity to use your vacation home for a handful of days?"

Rich was happy to offer up his beautiful place for a week when it was empty, and my family had an amazing time, thanks to him. Another friend did the same huge favor for me and my family with his house in Colorado. Minutes away from South Park, the namesake for the TV show. We have unforgettable stories from both trips.

You may have heard the phrase "beg, borrow, or steal," which means you'll get it by any means necessary. I like the passion and determination behind that phrase, but I'd rather skip the jail time. So I swapped "steal" for "deal." Here are a few creative ways to get what you want without spending any money.

Beg

This strategy sounds negative, because no one wants to beg. But really, it's just asking for what you want. You could ask someone you know or post your request in an online "pay nothing" or "buy nothing" group. Many people want to get rid of things they don't need or want anymore and are happy to give it a good home. When asking, always give the person you are asking an easy out so as not to burden them. I often will start by saying, "I have an ask, but please know I have no expectations. And a no is a-okay..."

Borrow

The day I bought my first pickup truck, my friend said, "Everyone is going to want to borrow it." Guess what? Almost no one asks. I borrowed Rich's Vermont vacation home way back when. And even though I can afford one of my own, I borrowed my workout buddy Art Muti's chain saw to cut up some fallen trees. Actually, I borrowed Art too. He wanted to operate the chain saw (I guess he saw me coming). We had a great afternoon cutting up dead trees together. If you don't plan to use something more than a few times, don't buy one of your own—borrow one instead. Did you know your local library lends other stuff besides books? You can get museum passes, kitchen tools and equipment, and so much more.

Deal

Do you have something of value, and can you strike an exchange with someone to get what you want? An example of this is a house exchange. I wanted a place to stay when we traveled internationally, so we made a deal to swap houses with another family. The deal we agreed to was to stay at their home, and they would visit the United States at the same time and stay at ours. Not only did we have free lodging; we also got a free house sitter. Then COVID scratched that plan, but future house swaps are in the works. You'll find house exchange and barter communities online. Just be sure to do your homework before you commit.

Gamify Saving for Big Purchases

As I write this, I'm saving to buy a new twelve-string guitar. I don't need it—I want it. And at around $1,000 it's not cheap, at least not to me. So I set up a bank account labeled D-Guitar. Then, I bought an eight-dollar, hundred-piece LEGO guitar set, as in you build the guitar out of LEGO pieces. First, I put in the eight dollars into the D-Guitar account for the set. Then, for every ten dollars I save, I add one piece to the guitar. When I add fifty dollars, that's five pieces. As I save for the guitar, I see the LEGO version coming to life right in front of me. The day the set is built, I will purchase my guitar and jam out the ultimate twelve-string treat: Pink Floyd's "Wish You Were Here."

Saving for a big purchase in the distant future can feel like you'll never get there, so find a way to gamify the process with a visual or other sensory representation of your goal. This leverages the behavioral tendency of dopamine reinforcement, where tracking progress visually or tangibly (ideally both) keeps you engaged with the frequent satisfying feedback. How can you see your progress grow? Here are a couple of ideas.

Use a Map

For a dream vacation, tack a map onto corkboard and draw a line between where you live and where you want to go. Then, determine the distance in miles. Assign a dollar amount for each mile and add a pushpin to the map for every one hundred miles, or whatever number makes sense. Watch as you get closer and closer to your destination.

Piece Together the Puzzle

For the new TV in my workout room, I marked the spot on the wall with painter's tape. Then, I cut up a picture of Arnold Schwarzenegger's robot character into ten pieces. Every $25 I saved earned me a piece of the picture, which I added to the taped box. After saving $250 and completing the "puzzle," I ordered the TV. This time I watched the original *Terminator*. I'm classy like that.

Use a Fitting Representation

For a down payment on a house, you could try the LEGO idea, or the stones in a jar method. Assign a dollar value for each stone and watch it fill up as your savings grows. If it's a beach house, fill it with seashells. A lake house, use cork stoppers. A cabin in the woods, acorns. You get the drift.

Avoid Impulse Purchases While Shopping in Person

It happens to all of us. We go to the store with one goal in mind and come home with a trunk full of stuff we didn't know we needed. (Pro tip: We didn't need any of it.) Here are a few tips to help you avoid impulse purchases when you're out and about.

Use Gift Cards

Lock away your credit cards and use gift cards for essential purchases. This limits your spending to what's on the card, preventing unnecessary splurges. Avoid auto-replenishing the balance, as that defeats the purpose. Be mindful of any remaining balances and don't let them go to waste. Check if the store can cash out the difference, or use the leftover amount toward another purchase, like groceries. Lastly, steer clear of gift cards with expiration dates or inactivity fees to ensure you get the most value.

Shop the Outer Edge

Most grocery stores will have everything you need on the edges of the store, such as produce and meats. The stuff you use most often, like dairy products, will strategically be in the most distant corner from the entrance. This design forces you to walk deeper into the store, through the junk food aisles. Stay on the edge, and don't shortcut through the aisles.

Use a List

This technique seems pretty basic, but it's wildly effective. Decide what you need in advance and purchase only the items on your list. Bring a pen to check off the item you intended to get when you put it in the cart. Feeling tempted by something shiny? Write it down on your list anyway with the name, price, and a big frowny face next to it. That small act of pausing and labeling it as an emotional buy often kills the desire on the spot. Impulse buying be damned!

Bring Your Own Bags

Some stores either require you to pay for your bags or give you a discount if you bring your own bags. When you limit your purchases to what can fit in your bags, you are less likely to purchase things that aren't on your list. Smaller bags will result in smaller purchases.

Use the Smaller Cart

You can apply the small bag method at the grocery store and at big box stores. The bigger the cart, the more you are likely to purchase. So choose the smallest cart available. Or stick your kid in there. The space they take up reduces purchases, as their grubby hands grabbin' for Froot Loops can have a counter effect.

Play the "Just One More Day" Game

If you still feel tempted to purchase something you didn't plan on buying at the store, tell yourself you can/need to wait "just one more day." You can come back the next day to get it if you like. By doing this, you break the pattern of the impulse buy. And if you still want it the next day, go back and get it. (You probably won't.)

Pay for Everything with a Twenty-Dollar Bill

Cash isn't as popular as it once was, but it still works well in so many ways. I used to pay for everything with twenty-dollar bills. So when I bought something for seven dollars, I would break out a twenty from my wallet in my right pocket. The change would go in my left pocket. A nineteen-dollar purchase would put one dollar in my left pocket. A purchase of thirty-three dollars would require two twenty-dollar bills to cover and would leave seven dollars for the left pocket. Then at the end of the day, when I was getting changed for bed, the left pocket funds would go into a Fun account. I filled my wallet only with one hundred dollars (five twenties) a week. So I was cautious in spending it. And it forced more thoughtful spending. If I saw a York Peppermint Patty at a store, I would be less tempted to buy it because it could "cost me" a twenty. And when I did go shopping, I would bundle shopping to be efficient.

Adjust Technology to Make It Harder to Shop

Nicole Chiarolla participated in the Money Habit training at A1 Garage Door Service and found a way to work *with* her online shopping habit, rather than try to eliminate it. She would put items in her online shopping cart, just as she always did. But rather than checkout that day, she waited more than "just one day"—she waited at least two weeks. Anything she still wanted at that time she would purchase. Online "window shopping" gave her the same serotonin rush she got from checking out, and she didn't buy as much stuff. This helped Nicole save enough to pay an additional $700 per month on her mortgage.

You can use technology to your advantage, to work with your habits. Here are a few ideas.

Turn Off Notifications

If you get notifications from retailers—turn them off! You don't need reminders to buy stuff. You can handle that on your own.

Add Friction

Make it harder to shop. Put your favorite shopping app in a hidden folder on your phone. Or better yet, delete it entirely. It's easy enough to go the retailer's website. Also, remove your payment information from retailer's sites so you'll have to manually enter it every time. And sign in as a guest; don't set up an account.

Don't Store Passwords in Your Browser

If you do want to keep your online shopping accounts, to keep points or to get special deals, don't store your passwords in your browser. Make it harder to login by storing your passwords in a hidden location or an external password system that won't autofill.

Swap the Cart for a Wish List

Nicole likes the shopping cart method, but you can take it one step further and add your items to a wish list. Transferring wish list items to your cart adds another step, which gives you one more chance to decide if you really want it. And if someone wants to know what to get you for a gift, you can easily send them your wish list.

Delay Shipping

Choose delayed shipping time for online purchases so you have time to cancel the order before it ships. This gives you even more time to reconsider your purchase.

Negotiate Better Deals and Rates

Many people don't realize fees and rates are not fixed; most companies will negotiate with you to keep you as a customer. Here are a few techniques to try.

Cable Television

Research alternative services in your area. Call your current provider and ask them to lower the price. Tell them you are prepared to switch to the other service. Always try to be in a position of power and have the alternative ready to go.

Cell Phones

You will likely see offers or promotions for other phone plans that are cheaper than yours. Do a bit of research. Then, call your current provider and ask if they can match or beat the competitor's offer. Mention that you're considering switching carriers but would prefer to stay if they can provide a better deal. Providers often have retention offers they don't advertise. If they don't budge, consider switching or as we learned from Dom Anderson early on, revisit the negotiation in a week or in an hour—it might land you a better deal with a different customer representative.

Mortgage

If the current interest rates are lower than your mortgage rate, you may want to refinance. But watch out for hidden costs. Sometimes fees are buried in your new mortgage payment, and you don't realize it because it's lower than your current payment. Except you'll be paying the mortgage for a longer period. Do the math—are you truly paying less over time? If so, then refinancing is often worth doing.

Negotiation Swap

Sometimes it's easier to be tough in negotiations when it's not your account. Get a friend to swap calls with you—they handle your negotiations, and you handle theirs. Or if you're not great at conflict or at holding your ground, get one of your "tougher" friends to negotiate on your behalf and offer to help them in some other way. I had my friend Vito make a call for me once. He is a softy and sucks at negotiations. But when he said, "My name is Vito. And I am calling on behalf of my good palsy-walsy Mike Michalowicz…" he didn't need to say anything more. The deal was done.

Work with Your Employer to Save More

Here are some tips to help you save more with your employer's help.

Payday Every Two Weeks

If you get paid every two weeks, there will be two months in a year that you get a third paycheck that month. Put all that money into your FUTURE account or to pay off FIX. Or based on your season, put it into DREAMS or WANTS. The thing is, you have adjusted to live off two pay checks per month. So the two "extras" feel like a bonus and should be treated that way.

Sign Up for a Retirement Plan

If your employer has a 401(k) or another form of retirement savings, participate in it! This is pretax savings. I strongly encourage you to go for the maximum contribution (typically 15 percent of your income), but you can start smaller and work your way up to it. This is called a step-up plan, where your employer automatically increases your contribution every year. If you haven't participated in a company retirement plan before, it can feel painful in the moment. But consider it a financial workout; you will adjust and get stronger. Plus, you should have been doing it before, so this is a catch-up.

Ask Your Employer to Match Your Contribution

Some employers match your retirement contribution up to a certain percentage (typically 5 percent). This is free money! Free money, I tell you. For all that is holy, put down this book, and get on that program now.

Put Half Your Raise in Retirement

When you get a raise, put 50 percent of that raise toward your 401(k) contribution on a percentage basis.

Get an Alternative Retirement Plan

If you don't have access to a 401(k) or another form of retirement savings through your employer, find one of the different forms of individual retirement accounts (IRAs) and put money there.

Work with Your Bank to Save More

Here are some ways to save more with your bank's help.

Set Up a CD Ladder

I learned about Certificates of Deposit (CDs) and CD ladders in college in my finance class. It worked back in the early '90s, and it works now. The idea is to put money in a CD account that yields higher interest than a savings account but also restricts your access by holding the funds for a specific period. Say you have $20,000 in your EMERGENCY account. You want to earn more but also have the flexibility of pulling from it quickly when you need to. You would put $5,000 in a three-month CD, another $5,000 in a six-month CD, $5,000 in a nine-month CD, and $5,000 in a one-year CD.

When the three-month CD matures, renew it in as an annual. Do the same annual renewal with each subsequent maturing CD. That way, every three months, money is available (the $5,000 plus interest earned). If you don't need it, renew it for another year. This way you always have $5,000 (plus interest) within three months and $10,000 within six months (if you don't renew the previous three-month CD).

Use a Slow Bank Transfer

Set up a savings account in a separate bank that takes two to three days for transfers. When you move money there, it's not easily accessible for impulsive spending.

Automatically Round It Up

See if your bank offers to round up your debit card payments to the next dollar and automatically put that money into a retirement (FUTURE) or DREAM account.

These money-saving strategies aren't about playing games, being gimmicky, or coming up with cute tricks. They are about allowing yourself to be unapologetically you. The truth is, your habits are powerful. When you align your financial controls with your natural tendencies, you tap into your greatest strength—your ability to work with who you are, not against it. These tips and hacks are tools to channel your instincts in a way that builds your confidence and momentum, one small but meaningful step at a time.

I hope you are realizing that you are capable of so much more than just keeping up—you are proving you can get ahead and stay there. By gamifying your savings, managing subscriptions, and negotiating better deals, you're proving to yourself that financial success isn't about sacrifice or deprivation. It's about creativity, control, and claiming the freedom to live life on your terms. Cherry-pick the ideas from this section that feel right. You don't have to change who you are. In fact, you shouldn't. Instead, unlock the power of who you already are.

Notes

Chapter 1: You Have (Already) Won the Lottery

p. 8 *the most common jackpot amounts:* "Mega Millions Prizes," Mega-Millions.com, accessed June 11, 2025, mega-millions.com/prizes.

p. 9 *the infamous story of Jack Whittaker:* John Raby, "From Powerball Winner to Scandal: Jack Whittaker Dies at 72," KOIN, June 30, 2020, koin.com/news/national/from-powerball-winner-to-scandal-jack-whittaker-dies-at-72.

p. 11 *This approach aligns with cognitive load theory: Cognitive Load Theory: A Guide to Applying Cognitive Load Theory to Your Teaching,* Medical College of Wisconsin Office of Educational Improvement (May 2022), mcw.edu/-/media/MCW/Education/Academic-Affairs/OEI/Faculty-Quick-Guides/Cognitive-Load-Theory.pdf.

p. 19 *80 percent of New Year's resolutions fail:* Dr. Kevin Campbell, "How to Make Big Health Gains in the New Year," *U.S. News & World Report,* January 5, 2018, health.usnews.com/health-care/for-better/articles/2018-01-05/how-to-make-big-health-gains-in-the-new-year.

p. 20 *budgets work about as well as diets:* Yoni Freedhoff, "No, 95 Percent of People Don't Fail Their Diets," *U.S. News & World Report,* November 17, 2014, health.usnews.com/health-news/blogs/eat-run/2014/11/17/no-95-percent-of-people-dont-fail-their-diets.

p. 20 *"There's a conscious part that you think of":* Howard Farkas, *8 Keys to End Emotional Eating* (W.W. Norton & Company, 2019).

Chapter 2: The Money Habit System

p. 32 *We focus most on what's right in front of us:* Shane Frederick, "Cognitive Reflection and Decision Making," *Journal of Economic Perspectives* 19, no. 4 (Fall 2005): 25–42, doi.org/10.1257/089533005775196732.

p. 35 "Sometimes the most advanced thing you can do": Ramit Sethi, *I Will Teach You to Be Rich: No Guilt. No Excuses. Just a Six-Week Program That Works*, 2nd ed. (Workman Publishing Co., 2019).

p. 40 *Phillippa Lally's habit formation study:* "Phillippa Lally and the Number of Days to Form a Habit," The Science of Self-Help, July 26, 2013, scienceofselfhelp.org/articles-1/phillippa-lally-and-the-number-of-days-to-form-a.

Chapter 3: Align Your Money Target With Your Financial Season

p. 44 *A staggering 133,223 bankruptcy filings:* Bankruptcy Filing Trends in California (American Bankruptcy Institute, February 2024), abi-org.s3.amazonaws.com/Newsroom/State_Filing_Trends/2024/Filing_Trends_California.pdf.

p. 62 *people often experience greater anxiety waiting:* David B. Portnoy, "Waiting Is the Hardest Part: Anticipating Medical Test Results Affects Processing and Recall of Important Information," Social Science & Medicine 71, no. 2 (May 5, 2010): 421–28, doi.org/10.1016/j.socscimed.2010.04.012.

p. 65 *"putting things into people's heads is the sure way":* Dictionary of National Biography, vol. 17 (1889), "Elwes, John."

p. 65 *In her book* High Agency Human: Vickie Lanthier, *High Agency Human: Navigate Adversity and Live Big* (pub. by author, 2025).

Chapter 6: Crush Your Debt

p. 125 *the massive credit card debt Americans carry:* Matt Schulz, "2025 Credit Card Debt Statistics," LendingTree, January 9, 2025, lendingtree.com/credit-cards/study/credit-card-debt-statistics.

p. 136 *psychologists George Ainslie and Richard Herrnstein:* Till Grüne-Yanoff, "Models of Temporal Discounting 1937–2000: An Interdisciplinary Exchange Between Economics and Psychology," Science in Context 28, no. 4 (December 2015): 675–713, doi.org/10.1017/s0269889715000307.

p. 137 *explained by optimal foraging theory:* "Optimal Foraging," ScienceDirect, accessed June 11, 2025, sciencedirect.com/topics/medicine-and-dentistry/optimal-foraging.

Chapter 7: Build a Better Financial Future Now

p. 141 *"As a species, we haven't evolved to plan":* Benjamin Hardy, *Be Your Future Self Now: The Science of Intentional Transformation* (Hay House, Inc., 2022).

p. 142 *A study documented by Berkley.edu revealed:* Brad M. Barber, Yi-Tsung Lee, Yu-Jane Liu, and Terrance Odean, "The Cross-Section of Speculator

Skill: Evidence from Day Trading," *Journal of Financial Markets* 18 (March 2014): 1–24, doi.org/10.1016/j.finmar.2013.05.006.

p. 144 *"Many investors fail to remain invested in stocks":* Nathan Reiff, "Benefits of Holding Stocks for the Long Term," Investopedia, updated October 29, 2024, investopedia.com/articles/investing/052216/4-benefits-holding-stocks-long-term.asp.

p. 153 *According to the Trinity study:* Jason S. Scott, William F. Sharpe, and John G. Watson, "The 4% Rule—At What Price?" *Journal of Investment and Management* 7, no. 3 (Third Quarter 2009): 1–24, web.stanford.edu/~wfsharpe/retecon/4percent.pdf.

p. 159 *"Time is what we want most":* William Penn, *Some Fruits of Solitude in Reflections and Maxims Relating to the Conduct of Human Life* (London: Printed for Thomas Northcott, 1693).

Chapter 8: Embrace Your New Identity

p. 165 *money is one of the top reasons couples argue:* "Happy Couples: How to Avoid Money Arguments," American Psychological Association, 2015, apa.org/topics/money/conflict.

Conclusion: Go Get Your Moments

p. 177 *people often experience higher anxiety:* Kate Sweeny and Arezou Ghane Cavanaugh, "Waiting Is the Hardest Part: A Model of Uncertainty Navigation in the Context of Health News," *Health Psychology Review* 6, no. 2 (2010): 147–64, doi.org/10.1080/17437199.2010.520112.

Appendix: Tips and Hacks to Save More Money

p. 185 *average American spends $219 per month:* "Subscription Service Statistics and Costs," C+R Research, updated July 26, 2024, crresearch.com/blog/subscription-service-statistics-and-costs.

Index

Figures are indicated by page numbers in *italics*

A1 Garage Door Service, 1–2, 5
accountability, 33
Activate season: about, 48–49, 60, 81; investing goals, 151; Money Target allocations, *53–55*; unpredictable income and, 57–58
affordability test, 113
agency, regaining, 65–66
Ainslie, George, 136
Aliche, Tiffany, 63–64, 68
American Dream, 1, 6, 152
amount, savings, 10–12, *10*, 148
analysis paralysis, 114–15
Anderson, Dom, 119–21, 133–34, 138–39
asset-based debt, 88–89
attentional bias, 32
automatic payments: account allocations, 30, 35, 117; credit cards, 188; investments, 144, 159; round it up, 198
autonomy, vs. control, 20–21, 99, 166
avalanche method, debt, 130–32, *131*, 140

bags, grocery, 193
Balance season: about, 49–50, 60, 81; author's experience, 50, 110–11, *110*; Money Target allocations, *53–55*
bank accounts: allocations example, *34*; automatic transfers, 30, 35, 117; disbursement rhythm, 33–35; fees, 40, 46; hiding from view, 94, 105, 117; interest-yielding accounts, 148, 151; labeling, 68, 97; Money Target allocations, 53, *53–55*, 55; multiple accounts, 29–30, *31*, 32–33, 66–67; One Account Challenge, 35–38, 41; overcomplication, 114; removing temptation, 32–33; setting up, 38–40, 41; tips, 197–98. *See also* clarity accounts; DREAMS account; EMERGENCY account; FIX/FUTURE account; INCOME account; Money Habit system; NEEDS account; WANTS account
bank balance budgeting, 19–21
bankruptcy, 44, 46
beg, 189
behavior: analysis paralysis, 114–15; attentional bias, 32; autonomy vs. control, 20–21, 99, 166; being present vs. financial anxiety, 173–80;

being too logical, 114; blaming the system, 115; cognitive distortion, 119–21; cognitive load, 11; conversations about money, 164–68, 171; decision-making, 141–42, 144; dopamine reinforcement, 127, 136–38, 191; emotions, 114, 161–64; false sense of security, 115; forgetfulness, 114; loss aversion, 154; magnification, 120–21; miser syndrome, 64–65; optimal foraging theory, 137; Parkinson's Law, 104, 124, 154; paying yourself first, 135–38; self-punishment, 138–40; status quo bias, 122; temporal discounting, 135–36; uncertainty and, 62, 111–13, 177–78. *See also* habits; stress

Be Your Future Self Now (Hardy), 141–42

big purchases, 47, 49, 94–95, 190–91. *See also* DREAMS account

blaming the system, 115

borrow, 190

budgeting systems: bank balance budgeting, 19–21; envelope system, 3, 28–29, 43–45, 67; problems with traditional tools, 99, 166

cable television, 195
Canyon Ranch, 94–95, 116
cars and car repairs, 106–7, *107*, 112, 133
carts, shopping, 193, 194–95
cash, using, 193
cash confidence, 5, 23–24, 25. *See also* confidence
cell phones, 195
Certificates of Deposit (CD) ladders, 197–98
charitable giving, 48
checking accounts, 38–39
Chiarolla, Nicole, 194
Christian Louboutin shoes, 170–71
chronometer, 51–52

clarity, 62–63, 66, 92
clarity accounts: about, 95; author's accounts, 100–101, *100*, 107–11, *108*, *109*, *110*; for big dreams, 93–95, 116; customizing, 102–5; financial uncertainty and, 111–13; NEEDS vs. WANTS, 106–7, *107*; next steps, 117; power of, 96–101, *100*; screwing up, 113–15; shopping and, 113. *See also* bank accounts
clothing, 77, 106, *107*, 170–71
cognitive distortion, 119–21
cognitive load, 11
college funds, 47
commitment devices, 124
compound interest, 144–48, *146*, *147*–48
confidence, 91, 129, 133–35. *See also* cash confidence
consistency, 56, 58, 157. *See also* frequency, savings
contribution matching, 144
control: vs. autonomy, 20–21, 99, 166; taking, 87, 91, 99
conversations, about money, 163–68, 171
credit cards: credit limits, 124–25, 187; interest rates, 125–26, 128; subscriptions and, 185–86; tips, 187–88, 192
credit scores and reports, 46, 187–88

deal, 190. *See also* negotiation
debit cards, 111, 187
debt: asset-based vs. liability-based, 88–89; debt avalanche method, 130–32, *131*, 140; debt collection, 15, 134–35, 138–39; debt freeze method, 121–26, 140; debt snowball method, 127–29, *129*, 140; FIX account for, 30, 32; within Money Habit system, 87–88; negotiating, 133–35; next steps, 140; Recover season and, 46, 60; self-punishment and, 138–40;

student loans, 46, 132; tax debt, 46; and WANTS and DREAMS, 135–38. *See also* credit cards; mortgage; Recover season
decision-making, 141–42, 144, 177. *See also* conversations, about money
deficit, 80, 81
deprivation, 135–37
dining out, 75–76, 77, 98. *See also* groceries
disbursement rhythm, 33–35
discretionary spending. *See* WANTS account
dollar-cost average system, 143, 159
dopamine reinforcement, 127, 136–38, 191
down payments, 47, 60, 105. *See also* housing; mortgage; rent
DREAMS account: about, 30, *31*, 32, 38, 77; automatic round-ups, 198; clarity accounts and, 98; don't sacrifice, 135–38; financial seasons and, 60; inflation and, 90; reflection questions, 85, 86. *See also* big purchases
Dugger, Amber, 83, 87, 99, 123

Elwes, John, 65
EMERGENCY account: about, 30, *31*, 32, 38, 77; clarity accounts and, 98, 101; Fund season and, 47; inflation and, 90; reflection questions, 86; Rent account as, 103, 105
emergency expenses, 12–14, 23–24
emotions, 114, 161–64. *See also* dopamine reinforcement
employers, 196–97
entertainment, *107*. *See also* subscriptions
entrepreneurship, 47, 48
envelope system, 3, 28–29, 43–45, 67
expenses: big purchases, 47, 49, 94–95, 190–91; cutting, 122–23; general spending, 104, 105; tracking monthly spending, 74–78, *75, 76, 78, 92*; unexpected, 12–14, 23–24. *See also* NEEDS account; WANTS account

facing facts, 83, 92, 140
Farkas, Howard, 20–21, 166
fear. *See* emotions; uncertainty
fees, bank, 40, 46
finances. *See* money
financial freedom, 27, 64, 152–59, 170–71, 179–80
financial seasons: adapting to, 59–61; Money Map and, 81–82, *82*; Money Target allocations by, 53–56, *53–55*; next season, 50–51; next steps, 68; overview, 45–50; regaining agency, 65–67; regular review, 56. *See also* Activate season; Balance season; Fund season; Recover season
FIX/FUTURE account: about, 30, 31–32, *31*, 38, 53, 77; automatic round-ups, 198; clarity accounts and, 98; financial seasons and, 59–60; negotiation and, 135; reflection questions, 85–87; removing temptation, 32–33
food (groceries), 77, 106, *107*, 111, 192–93. *See also* dining out
foreclosure, 46
forgetfulness, 114
4 percent rule, 153, 156
401(k) program, 33, 47, 144, 196–97
freeze method, debt, 121–26, 140
frequency, savings, 10–12, *10*, 148–52, *149–51*. *See also* consistency
friction, adding, 194
friends, 168–70, 196
frugality, 64–65
Fund season: about, 47, 60, 81; author's experience, 109, *109*; investments during, 151; Money Target allocations, *53–55*

FUTURE account. *See* FIX/FUTURE account
Future You account, 159

gamification, 190–91
general spending, 104, 105
gift cards, 192
goals: financial seasons and, 47, 60; investments, 148–52, *149–51*
groceries (food), 77, 106, *107*, 111, 192–93. *See also* dining out

habits: credit card alignment with, 187–88; development, 40–41; life changes and, 45; working with, 3–4, 5, 198. *See also* behavior; Money Habit system
hangovers, financial, 46
Hardy, Benjamin P., 141–42
Harrison, John, 51–52
health: health insurance, 33, 44, 112; NEEDS VS. WANTS, 106, *107*; planning for long-term health care, 47; unexpected costs, 12–14, 23–24, 30, 162–64
Herrnstein, Richard, 136
hiding from view: bank accounts, 94, 105, 117; credit cards, 188
High Agency Human (Lanthier), 65–66
holidays. *See* vacations
Horton-Martin, Sam, 61–63, 68, 96–97
house exchange, 190
housing, 46, 49, 106, *107*. *See also* down payments; mortgage; rent

identity, 169–71
impulse purchases, avoiding, 192–93
income: financial freedom, 152–57; Money Target allocations by, 53, *53–55*; monthly usable income (MUI), 71–74, 72, 73, 92; unpredictable income, 56–58

INCOME account, 29, *31*, 32, 38–39
index funds, 143, 159
individual retirement accounts (IRAS), 197
indulgences, 48, 170–71. *See also* WANTS account
inflation, 89–90
inheritance. *See* windfalls
interest rates: credit cards and, 125–26, 128; debt avalanche method and, 130–32, *131*; debt snowball method and, 127
investments: automatic, 144, 159; compound interest, 144–48, *146*, *147–48*; in future self, 141–42, 159; goals and funding frequency, 148–52, *149–51*; interest-yielding bank accounts, 148, 151; living on interest only, 152–57, *155*; next steps, 159; online calculator, 152; winning strategies, 142–44. *See also* savings

"just one more day" game, 193

Lally, Phillippa, 40
Lanthier, Vickie, 65–66, 68
liability-based debt, 88–89
lifestyle upgrades, 48, 113. *See also* financial freedom
Lim, Donna, 43–45, 66–68
list, shopping, 192
loans, 46. *See also* debt
lockbox, with timer, 188
logical, being too, 114
loss aversion, 154
lotteries, 7–10, 142. *See also* windfalls
luxuries, 48, 170–71. *See also* WANTS account

magnification, 120–21
Manders, Rich, 157–59, 189, 190
medical expenses. *See* health
Mello, Tommy, 2, 5

minimum payments, 188
miser syndrome, 64–65
money: being present vs. financial anxiety, 173–80; conversations about, 163–68, 171; facing facts, 83, 92, 140; financial freedom, 27, 64, 152–59, 170–71, 179–80; financial hangovers, 46; financial trauma, 161–64; money shuffle, 16; not (always) the answer, 18–19; shame and, 91, 138–40
Money Habit system: about, 6, 22–23, 25, *31*, 91; acting today, 27–28; allocations example, *34*; amount and frequency of savings, 10–12, *10*, 148; author's experience, 25, 28; background, 2–3, 5–6, 22; vs. bank balance budgeting, 19–21; blaming the system, 115; cash confidence and, 5, 23–24, 25; customizing, 105; vs. lotteries, 7–10; next steps, 41; sixty-six days to learn, 40–41. *See also* bank accounts; clarity accounts; debt; financial freedom; financial seasons; investments; Money Map; Money Target; savings
Money Map: about, 70, 71; calculation and analysis process, 79–85, *80*, *82*, *83*, *84*; inflation and, 89–90; monthly spending, 74–78, *75*, *76*, *78*, 92; monthly usable income (MUI), 71–74, *72*, *73*, 92; next steps, 92; online calculator, 85; self-reflection, 85–87
Money Target: about, 52, 68; allocations by financial season, 53–56, *53–55*; review, 56, 92; unpredictable income and, 56–58; when it feels out of reach, 58–59
monthly usable income (MUI), 71–74, *72*, *73*, 92
mortgage: inflation and, 90; as NEED vs. DREAM, 77; negotiating, 195–96; reverse mortgages, 153, 154; term origins, 140. *See also* down payments; housing; rent

NEEDS account: about, 29, *31*, 32, 38–39, 77; clarity accounts and, 97–98; Fund season and, 47; inflation and, 89, 90; reflection questions, 85, 86; vs. WANTS, 106–7, *107*
neglect, 114
negotiation, 133–35, 195–96. *See also* deal
notifications, turning off, 194

One Account Challenge, 35–38, 41
online shopping, 194–95
optimal foraging theory (OFT), 137
overcomplication, 114
overdraft fees, 46
overwhelm, 11–12, 24, 36, 65, 114–15, 119

Parkinson's Law, 104, 124, 154
passwords, storing, 194
Penn, William, 159
personal finance: author's rock bottom, 14–18; bank balance budgeting, 19–21; envelope system, 3, 28–29, 43–45, 67; more money not (always) the answer, 18–19; (somewhat) working systems, 115; traditional budgeting tools, 99, 166; unexpected expenses, 12–14, 23–24. *See also* Money Habit system
personal growth, 48
philanthropy, 48
Piper, Carol, 168–70
present, being, 173–80
Profit First (Michalowicz), 2, 4
Profit First system, 3–4, 22, 66–68, 135
property investment, 47
puzzles, piecing together, 191

quarterly check-ins, 56, 115

Radical Reduction, 65–66
Rainy Day fund, 47. *See also*
   EMERGENCY account; Fund season
Ramsey, Dave, 127
Recover season: about, 46, 81;
   author's experience, 108–9, *108*;
   clarity through focus, 63; Donna
   Lim's experience, 43–45, 66–68;
   indicators for, 60; Money Target
   allocations, *53–55*; oversaving,
   64–65; priorities, 59; regaining
   agency, 65–66; Sam Horton-
   Martin's experience, 61–63, 68,
   96–97; starting with, 56
relationships: conversations about
   money, 163–68, 171; friends,
   168–70, 196
renovations, home, 49
rent, 37, 90, 98, 103. *See also* down
   payments; housing; mortgage
repossession, 46
representative items, 191
restaurant meals, 75–76, 77, 98.
   See also groceries
retirement: employer's help,
   196–97; financial freedom, 152–57;
   401(k) program, 33, 47, 144,
   196–97; Fund season and, 47;
   individual retirement accounts
   (IRAS), 197; time/money
   inversion, 157–59
reverse mortgages, 153, 154
review, financial, 56, 58–59, 92, 114
rhythm, financial, 33–35, 50
rounding up, automatic, 198
Ruta, Kelly, 166–68

sacrifices, 135–38
Saddler, Kari, 38
savings: amount, 10–12, *10*, 148;
   financial freedom, 27, 64, 152–59,
   170–71, 179–80; frequency, 10–12,
   10, 148–52, *149–51*; goals, 148–52,
   149–51; oversaving, 64–65; savings

accounts, 38. *See also* FIX/FUTURE
   account; investments
seasons. *See* financial seasons
secured debt, 88
security, false sense of, 115
self-criticism, 81
self-punishment, 138–40
Sethi, Ramit, 35
"set it and forget it," 115, 142. *See also*
   automatic payments
75 percent rule, 153–54, 156–57
shame, 91, 138–40
shipping, delaying, 195
shopping: big purchases, 47, 49, 94–95,
   190–91; gamification, 190–91;
   impulse control while in-person,
   192–93; technological barriers while
   online, 194–95; Try It First rule, 113
side hustles, 47, 111, 112
Simon & Garfunkel: "The Sound of
   Silence," 174
Skinner, B.F., 127
slow bank transfers, 198
snowball method, debt, 127–29, *129*,
   140
Snyder, Travis, 1, 5, 6
Social Security, 50, 72, 153
spending, monthly, 74–78, *75*, *76*, *78*,
   92. *See also* expenses
spontaneous spending, 49
sporadic expenses, 75–76
Stafford, Justin, 102–5
status quo bias, 122
stock market, 142–44. *See also*
   investments
streaming services, 112–13, 186–87
stress: being present vs. financial
   anxiety, 173–80; clarity accounts and,
   97–99, 104–5; financial seasons and,
   60; uncertainty and, 62, 177–78;
   unexpected expenses, 12–14, 23–24
student loans, 46, 132
subscriptions, 112–13, 185–87
survival, 57, 137

tax debt, 46
television, cable, 195
temporal discounting, 135–36
temptation, removing, 32–33, 117
Thoreau, Henry David, 15
time/money inversion, 48, 157–59
tinnitus, 173–75, 178–79, 180
The Total Money Makeover (Ramsey), 127
transportation, 106–7, *107*. *See also* cars and car repairs
trauma, financial, 161–64
truth, moment of, 83, 92, 140
Try It First rule, 113
twenty-dollar bills, 193

uncertainty, 62, 111–13, 177–78
unexpected expenses, 12–14, 23–24. *See also* EMERGENCY account
unpredictable income, 56–58
unsecured debt, 88–89

vacations, 30, 93–95, 98, 116, 138, 189, 191
vision boards, 93–95
Vivaldi, Antonio: "The Four Seasons," 45

WANTS account: about, 29, *31*, 32, 38, 77; clarity accounts and, 98; don't sacrifice, 135–38; financial seasons and, 60; Fund season and, 47; inflation and, 90; vs. NEEDS, 106–7, *107*; reflection questions, 85, 86; subscriptions and, 112–13
wealthy weekday, 41
Werner, Rachel, 165–66
Whittaker, Jack, 9
windfalls, 156, 157. *See also* lotteries
wish list, shopping, 194–95

PHOTO **MAT ROBINSON**

About the Author

BY HIS THIRTY-FIFTH BIRTHDAY, Mike Michalowicz (pronounced mi-'kal-o-wits) had founded and sold two multimillion-dollar companies. Confident that he had the formula to success, he became a small business angel investor and proceeded to lose his entire fortune. Then he started all over again, built three new multimillion-dollar companies, and committed to a new mission: Eradicate money struggles. Mike has devoted his life to the research, testing, and delivery of innovative, impactful strategies to achieve financial independence.

Mike is the host of the TV program *4-Minute Money Maker*. He is the creator of Profit First, considered the most popular small business cash management system in the world. *Profit First*, his book based on the system, has sold over one million copies (both editions) and is translated into thirty languages. Mike is also a former small business columnist for *The Wall Street Journal*. He is a main stage keynote speaker on innovative financial strategies and entrepreneurial topics.

Mike is the author of *All In, Get Different, Fix This Next, Clockwork, Surge, Profit First, The Pumpkin Plan, The Toilet Paper Entrepreneur*, and a children's book, *My Money Bunnies*. He lives in New Jersey.

Spread the Word

One Favor? Okay, Maybe Seven.

Has this book given something of value? Are you inspired to help me spread the word?

I'd be honored if you did even one or two of these. But if you went for all of them? I might do a cartwheel, and I don't even *do* cartwheels.

- ☑ Rate the book on your favorite audio platform.
- ☑ Review the book at your favorite online retailer.
- ☑ Sign up for the Money Habit newsletter at mymoneyhabit.com.
- ☑ Share passages and quotes from the book on social media.
- ☑ Share the book with a friend.
- ☑ Tell the boss to make this a book study for your company.
- ☑ And, if you are the boss, make it the book study for your company. I have guided options at, yup, mymoneyhabit.com.

Thank you for even considering supporting me in these ways. But no pressure at all if you decide to pass. What matters most is that *you* achieve worry-free financial independence. That's the ultimate win for you, for me, and for our world.

Want to Connect?

Loved *The Money Habit*? Let's keep the momentum going.

Get weekly wealth wisdom

Join my newsletter for bite-sized insights, money moves, and more:
mymoneyhabit.com

Hire me to speak at your event or work with your team

mikemichalowicz.com/speaking

Want books for your team or company?

We offer bulk pricing and even co-branded versions of *The Money Habit*.
books@mikemichalowicz.com

Want to interview me for your podcast, blog, or publication?

interview@mikemichalowicz.com

Need a Money Habit Friendly Bank?

This is the bank I personally use and have since partnered with:

DREAM FIRST BANK

No fees, built in support for The Money Habit, including Money Habit debit cards. Plus, the bank's name is DREAM FIRST. I mean, come on! Could it be any more perfect?!?!?

Ever Dream of Becoming a Published Author?

I know how overwhelming it can feel. I've lived the experience. The uncertainty, the doubt—it's all part of the journey. With the right guidance, you can go from idea to reality. Start here:

don't write *that* book!

Every author needs a team... and this is yours. With expert guidance from Mike Michalowicz and AJ Harper, *Don't Write That Book* gives you the clarity, tools, and support to craft the book only you can write (and readers can't wait to read).

dontwritethatbookpodcast.com

PAGE TWO SIMPLIFIED

Love big ideas but hate overcomplication? That's exactly why we built Simplified. Books published under this new imprint, a collaboration between Mike Michalowicz and Page Two, break down the toughest business and life challenges into clear, doable steps you can use right away.

pagetwosimplified.com

Got a book idea you can't shake? Penned With Purpose helps authors turn inspiration into impact. From workshops to full-service literary agent support, we guide you from first draft to published book so your words reach the readers who need them most.

mikemichalowicz.com/penned-with-purpose

Ever Dream of Starting Your Own Business?

Master every stage of your entrepreneurial journey with practical, game-changing strategies that drive success at every level.

The Toilet Paper Entrepreneur
toiletpaperentrepreneur.com

Profit First
profitfirstbook.com

The Pumpkin Plan
pumpkinplan.com

Surge
surgebymikemichalowicz.com

Get Different
gogetdifferent.com

Fix This Next
fixthisnext.com

Clockwork
clockworkbymikemichalowicz.com

All In
allinbymike.com

PHOTO **MAT ROBINSON**

Bring Mike Michalowicz to Your Group!

Learn how to build better money habits, create financial peace, and inspire your group with stories and strategies that stick.

World-Class Storyteller

Practical Money Strategies

Relatable, Fun, Energizing

Unforgettable Lessons

Actionable Takeaways for Everyday Life

Mike Michalowicz is a bestselling author who makes money simple—and even fun. Whether it's for your book club, family reunion, faith-based group, workplace, or community event, Mike delivers practical, energizing talks on personal finance and entrepreneurship.

Hire Mike to Speak

Mike is exclusively represented by Go Leeward, the leading speaking event management firm.

Li Hayes

Phone: +1.203.314.2441 · Email: sid@goleeward.com

HireMikeToSpeak.com · GoLeeward.com

Get the Free Resources!

Looking for more? Check out the
free book resources—and much more—at
mymoneyhabit.com